GOD IS MY PLUMBER

AND OTHER CASUAL MIRACLES

Recognize the Miracles

God Is My Plumber and Other Casual Miracles

© Michael E. Uebelhack, 2021 All rights reserved

No part of this publication may be reproduced, stored in a retrieval system, or transmitted in any form or by any means—electronic, mechanical or photocopy, recording or any other—except for brief quotations in printed reviews, without the prior permission of the publisher.

ISBN: 978-1-7374256-0-1

For ordering information:

>   Uebelhack Publishing, LLC
>
>   P.O. Box 2891
>
>   Idaho Falls, Idaho 83403-2891
>
>   (208) 266-5568 a.k.a. (208) BOOK-LOV(ER)
>
>   www.GodIsMyPlumber.com

Bulk discounts available

Crypto currencies accepted

Printed by Falls Printing in Idaho Falls, Idaho, USA

Dedication

This is for you, my God. My Heavenly Father. My Creator. My Savior. My Everlasting Alpha & Omega.

I pray it is worthy of your assignment.

Acknowledgments

God gets the credit for the inspiration behind this book which could be a casual miracle in and of itself.

I want to give thanks to Mom and Pop for raising me to be a Christian. I also want to thank the many proofreaders and friends who offered their input and suggestions along the way. That would include Ethan and Linda, my therapists, Mary, and Monika my dearest friends, and my beloved daughters, Hannah, Tara, and Jaime.

Writing a book turned out to be the easy part when compared to designing the cover. Special thanks to Hannah Rose for bailing me out with her graphic arts skills in this department.

Also, thanks for the many "likes, hearts, and comments" from the readers of my God Is My Plumber Facebook page.

And I would be remiss if I didn't include my loyal buddies, Tocin (Oxytocin), my kitty who was nearly always on my lap & my constant companion, and Bruiser, my Lab, who remained faithfully by my side.

Lastly, thank you to my beautiful, loving, and patient wife, Lisa. For without her God-given wisdom, gentle guidance and endless contribution, this book may have never reached the finish line, nor would it read as smoothly as it does.
`

Table of Contents

- Psalm 102:18 1
  - The Kitchen Sink 2
  - Listen and He Will Speak 4
  - The Island 5
  - Chills 8
  - The Shower 9
  - Cuffed & Stuffed 10
  - God is My Searchlight 12
  - Build It! 15
  - Vacuum Cleaner 17
  - God is 'Our' Fireman 18
  - Ski Slope 20
  - River Baptism 22
- More Casual Miracles & A Dream 26
  - The Simple Truth 28
  - Worry versus Faith 47
- More Casual Miracles 50
  - River Baptism Miracle continued… Expanded Jesus sighting section! 50
- Casual Miracles as Told to me by Others 57
- Proof that the Bible is a Historical Document 65
  - My Testimony 65
- The Power of the Holy Spirit 82
- The Ending 92
  - The Sinner's Prayer 92
- References & Resources 96

Preface

𝕿his book is written for everyone, Christian and non-Christian. I believe everyone has a story or what I like to call "casual miracles." I have captured a few of mine as well as some from others in this book. God, in His perfect timing, always works things out.

Also, the Bible is proven to be a historical document and can be relied upon as such.

Lastly, the gifts and fruits of the Holy Spirit we are given as born-again believers in Christ Jesus are spelled out in great detail.

I hope you find this book helpful in making you more aware of the *casual miracles* in your life. And I hope you enjoy the musical element as well as I've tried to bring the book alive from various talented musicians. Just say to your favorite app, "Hey Alexa" or "Hey Google, play the song" next to: 🎵

Introduction

Psalm 102:18

The reasons why I authored this book, *God Is My Plumber and other Casual Miracles,* were many. First, God told me to. Not only once. And not only in a dream. But nearly every time I shared His message, He was in the background saying, "Mike, write down what you have just shared." I heard it. I knew it. And I couldn't ignore it. For whatsoever God asks of me, I will surely do. After all, dying for me was the most He could do. Living for Him is the least I can do. And then I ran across this verse, which, even after I'd obeyed and written the rough version, pretty much cemented the deal. The verse found in Psalm 102:18 reads: *Write down for the coming generation what the LORD has done so that people not yet born will praise him.* (Today's English Version, (TEV), renamed the Good News Translation).

By sharing God's miracles in my life, I wish to illustrate three things: One, you simply cannot explain them any other way. They are *too* coincidental. Two, they are signs that He cares and loves us. And three, God is a 'personal' God. For it says in Matthew 10:29-31 that not a sparrow falls without God knowing it and that He also numbers the hairs on our heads. We are worth more than many sparrows.

Don't get me wrong, it has never been my intent to minimize God by saying small miracles are all of which He is capable. I only wish to illustrate that He is a very personal God and is with us all the time by whatever means He chooses, as you'll come to realize as you read this book.

Casual Miracle #1

The Kitchen Sink

The title of this book came to me as a result of my kitchen sink, Casual Miracle #1 – if you will – which was clogged for four days, unclogging itself and drained 'on its own.' You tell me that's not a sign? It was to me! He is a very personal God and does things solely for you that would excite only you! (Or me in this instance.) I knew it was an answer to my prayers. "This is my child with whom I am well pleased."

Whenever something as simple as a clogged drain "fixes itself," I give glory to God. That is when I had the thought to start writing down many of the little miracles I've witnessed throughout the course of my life. What I discovered was the more credit I gave to God, the more I noticed these "little miracles" and perhaps more occurred since I started giving credit where credit was due. They started coming so rapidly it was hard keeping track of them all! It soon became all I was doing. I now know, beyond a shadow of a doubt, if you give

God the credit in your life for all the blessings, the more He will bless you.

🎵 *Miracles* by Colton Dixon

So, Him asking so little of me, and even giving me all the material, how much easier could it be? After all, I give Him the credit for showing me my path, my skill, and my ability. Why not honor Him by giving a part of it back to Him? This is what I call a "no-brainer".

It is my sincere hope that people will start recognizing the signs, miracles, and wonders in their own lives so they can start to believe there *is* a God and their lives will be the better for it. Some have called it *evidence that demands a verdict.* (Josh McDowell)

🎵 As I began writing this, I was listening to KLOVE (a national Christian music station) and the song, *10,000 Reasons* by Matt Redman began playing. Now, *to me*, that's a sign!

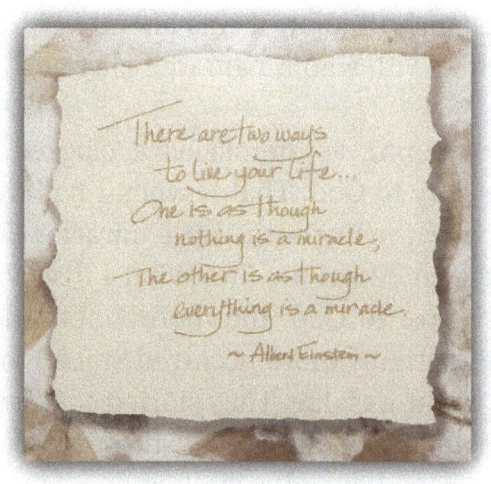

Speaking of listening...

Casual Miracle #2

Listen and He Will Speak

God is also my muse. When He unclogged my kitchen sink is when I decided to go ahead and write a book illustrating some of His miracles. So, I did.

Then, somehow, I lost the first chapter of this book. I had already written 1,000 words describing the story of just how the kitchen sink unclogged itself. I searched everywhere, high and low... couldn't find it. For the life of me, I couldn't find it anywhere. After much frustration and prayer for the safe return of my precious document, I stopped long enough to listen and realized that it didn't matter.

When I allowed God, my muse if you will, to speak, He told me I didn't need 1,000 words to describe the story. All the intricate details did not matter and, frankly, probably would not be that interesting to you. So see, He is already working in your life also, sparing you from possibly wasting your time. God is a God of miracles. After all, He did create everything. I don't really know if the seven days of creation were actually seven revolutions of the Earth spinning on its axis, but that is immaterial. He did it. I once saw a bumper sticker which I fully agree with. It read: *God Said It, I Believe it, End of Discussion.*

Then there was that time in Mauritius...

Casual Miracle #3

The Island

𝔄s a young Sailor, and after being at sea for many months, our ship anchored near the Island of Mauritius off the Southeast coast of Africa. While there, I frequented the Non-Commissioned Officers Club (NCOC) for some much-needed R&R.

After a few well-deserved beers, I decided to head back to the Ship on my own. Only my sense of direction, which was usually 180 degrees off anyways, proved true to form...

I even purposely hang out with people because they know the way back. This time, again, I went the wrong way. My thinking must have been, *well, I went left when I went in*, and that started an escalade of events. As I walked deep into the night, I started to realize that I was lost.

It was too late.

I couldn't find my way back to the NCO club to save myself. I was sunk. And no one that I knew—in their right mind—was anywhere near me. I got scared. I thought that my life was going to end that night. What did the locals think of American Sailors, I wondered? Here I was, white, and obviously did not belong there. I could not have even spoken to anyone beings they most likely did not speak a word of English. And hand signals... right. Give it up. All that was left for me was my God.

I didn't make any promises when I spoke to Him. I only asked for Him to save me. Not my soul, my situation! I prayed in silence, "God, I need some help here." And what happened next is nothing short of a miracle; as a matter of fact, I believe it was a miracle. I heard a voice in my head say, "Walk to that streetlamp and talk to the first person you see." That was it. Those were my instructions. So, I didn't ask any questions, I just walked to the light.

There was a young man at the light. He was alone and walking. I stopped him and said, "Hi, I am a Sailor and I can't find my ship." That must have sounded weird to him, but he didn't care. He said, "Well, I'm actually" (speaking English), "heading in the opposite direction, but I'll take you to your boat." I had a friend, (I hoped). He was a clean-cut young man that I felt like I could trust. Besides, this was an answer to a prayer!

As he walked, I followed him along a path that was very different than the one I had just used. The thought that he really wasn't taking me to the boat, crossed my mind. But perhaps he seemed to know a shortcut? We walked among other people, and as we did so, gangs split in two, and we walked right in the middle of them. We even walked under a bridge where other people were hanging out. I was nearly on his back so no one would talk to me.

We walked a long distance when finally, we came to the Liberty Boat. This was so relieving to me. I said thank you and asked if there was anything I could give him. He said, "Would you happen to have a cigarette?" Since I didn't smoke, I yelled into the Boat, "Hey, does anyone have a cigarette?" Would you believe that no one did! A boat full of Sailors, and I couldn't even get one lousy smoke to give to this guy who I felt had saved my life. So, I apologized to him and he said, "No problem," I climbed into the boat as he vanished into the night.

To this day, I believe that not only was that an answer to my Prayer, but that might have just been an Angel. Perhaps my Guardian Angel.

🎵 *Angels* by Amy Grant

This one experience has helped me keep my faith in the midst of all the nay-sayers, or times when I have thought God had abandoned me.

One of those times just happened to be...

Casual Miracle #4

Chills

At 12:40 a.m. I went out into our backyard and looked up and asked God to not abandon me. I am a sinner. It was not a typical full-version prayer. It was all I had left in me. And God knew it. No, "in Jesus' name I pray." No "Amen." Just, "God don't abandon me." And He spoke to me using the Holy Spirit who resides in me. Not just in my heart. But in every cell in my body. Within seconds, my entire body, from the top of my head to the tips of my fingers, all the way down to my toes, felt chills. I just hung my head and said, "Thank you." This continued for several minutes, and then I heard a silent "thought" say, "This is my child in whom I am well satisfied." And then another "thought", go in and write this down. When God talks to me, I listen and obey. That is why you are reading this. God will do this occasionally when you least expect it. And when it happens, you will feel no pain. It's as if He is healing you from your head to your toes.

God listens. And sometimes, especially when you are at your wit's end, He will answer your prayer immediately. You never know. Just don't give up on God. My God knows that I believe in Him 100%. No doubt. I know that when I leave this Earthly plane of existence, I will wake up in Heaven. Whenever and wherever that is. It will be like waking up from sedation after surgery. You won't know how long you were out. But you'll open your eyes, and you will be in Heaven. There's a song I would like to connect with this:

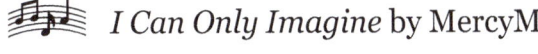   *I Can Only Imagine* by MercyMe

I remember the first time God emphatically talked to me...

Casual Miracle #5

The Shower

What started my path, and perhaps this book, was when I received my life's assignment from God Almighty. It happened while I was taking a shower as a teenager many years ago. It was another one of those inaudible messages similar to when I found myself lost on the Island of Mauritius, and God told me to "walk to the street light and talk to the first person you see." Many of you have heard the expression, *people will forget what you said or did, but they will never forget how you made them feel* by Maya Angelou. And that is why I've never forgotten that moment in the shower. He said life would not be easy for me so that I could relate to people of all color and from all walks of life. And He assured me that He would always be with me through it all; no matter what. And He has been. Our God keeps His promises. And I am trying to keep mine. That brings to mind this song:

🎵 *Nobody* by Casting Crowns... *Why you ever chose me has always been a mystery.*

The casual miracle is the moment in the shower. The fact that He has never let me down and has always been there for me are, I suppose, many more.

For I know the plans I have for you, declares the Lord, *plans to prosper you and not to harm you, plans to give you hope and a future.* – Jeremiah 29:11 (NIV)

It was then that I began listening to God and I have tried to do so throughout my life, especially during troubling times…

Casual Miracle #6

Cuffed & Stuffed

I had intended on reducing the insurance coverage on my car to only the required liability but had that "nagging feeling" one often gets when unsure of a course of action. I've come to learn to listen to these periods of uncertainty as a possible sign. When I feel or sense these moments in my life, I stop. And I will not continue on my present course until one, it becomes clear that everything is alright, or two, something happens where I could have really screwed things up for myself.

It was the first rainfall of the season making the streets slick and my car needed new tires anyway. After enjoying a beer with my burger and fries, I took a moment to relax before choosing a curvy back road and returning home. The reason why I had gone out and had dinner by myself was because the Misses and I had a little disagreement and I needed some time alone. The car I drove was no ordinary sedan but one where a little press on the gas-pedal prompted the horses under the hood to rear up and charge! Factor in all these components and you have a perfect storm. The rear-end broke loose and came around, and when all was said and done, the fiberglass car was no more. And neither were three trees.

Needless to say, officers were called to the scene and the resulting ordeal was nothing short of a fiasco. To make a long story short, I was tasered, wrestled to the ground, handcuffed, and arrested. I only wish everyone, including the rogue cop, were as in tune to God's messages as I am.

However, through it all, He protected me. My constant prayer was, "Help me, Jesus." And the scripture which helped me in the back of the cop car was, *Thou will keep thee in perfect peace whose mind is stayed on thee.* Isaiah 26:3. Oh, and did I mention that I have severe claustrophobia? The peace of God remained with me while being booked at the police station where they never put me in a holding cell but treated me with respect and decency. Part of this was due to being a Navy Veteran but mostly because I felt as if my best friend, Jesus, was right there beside me. He's always been with me during the most difficult times of my life.

The final result? I was never charged with a DUI or Resisting Arrest.

Oh, and by the way, 40 days after the incident, I received a check in the mail for over $8,500. That wouldn't have occurred if I didn't listen to my inner voice and held off on canceling full coverage insurance. The voice, I believe, is God speaking to me in however He does that sort of thing. You know what I'm talking about if you've ever "heard" it yourself. Sometimes God speaks to me through other people, which blesses not only me, but also them...

Casual Miracle # 7

God is My Searchlight

How's that? It's truly amazing. Here's the story, which is nothing short of a miracle.

The other evening, my daughter invited me over for dinner. She had made an extra stuffed pepper without mushrooms because she knows I'm not fond of them. The cool thing is that she didn't even know I was going to call, much less come over for dinner! So why did she make it in the first place? Hmm. It makes one wonder. So, I said, "sure, I'll ride down and have dinner with you." She said, "ride"? I said, "yea, I'm on the bike." Now, Jaime loves sitting on the back of my 1989 whisper-quiet Honda Goldwing and riding around the backcountry of these small towns in Idaho. I like to think she likes riding with her daddy and the bike is just an added bonus. Prior to this, we had a dispute going on, so it was a good time to resolve that little miscommunication. You all know that distance and time can cause families to think wrong things and cause that distance to grow in their minds. This is a horrible consequence of not staying in communication with the ones you love so dearly, especially family members. So, my instruction here is to: Call Your Mother and Your Father! And while you're at it, call your kids and your siblings. Don't let too much water flow under the bridge. So there. Having gotten that point across, here's the miracle part of the evening.

After dinner, we took off on the bike for a rather extensive ride under a smoggy half-moon. This time of year, and this year in particular, there are forest fires all around us in the Western part of the country. Add to that, the farmers are out cutting their hay and straw and bundling them for the winter feeding of their cows and horses. For the first half of the ride, the Sun was setting, and it was fairly warm and enjoyable. On our way back to her place, she showed me where her son, my grandson, would be catching the bus for his upcoming school year and then we rode to the school itself. It was there that she said, "uh-oh, I think I lost my phone." I said, "is it locked, or could someone just find your info and get it back to you?" She said, "no, but there are pictures on it that I really don't want to lose." I asked, "are they backed up?" She said, "no." To which I interjected, "Jesus Saves, and so should you." (This is a post-it note I have on my computers that my kids all know about). She asked if we could retrace our steps and try to find it. Well, by that time, it was totally dark. So I said, "if you can remember the route, we'll try." And off we went. Now by this time, the Sun was totally set, and the heat had left the countryside. So, we donned our Fall riding gear and headed off. And it was a good thing. For this time, all that straw and hay that the farmers were kicking up, and all those sprinkler systems seemed to all be timed to be hitting the road as we rode past. And did I mention the wind? For some reason, the wind started blowing like the Holy Spirit had finally reached this part of the World. The wind, sprinklers, hay, dust, dark, and everything else you can imagine were all against us.

While we are retracing our ride, going about 20 miles an hour, we took a turn that neither one of us thought was the way we had gone before. So, under an orange moon, we managed to manipulate the 800-pound bike, against the wind and got back on track. Of course, by now, I was praying that God would help us find her phone, mostly as a sign that He blesses those who love Him and keep His commandments. Now Jaime does a pretty good job at praying on her own, for she is by nature a pretty good kid. There was a song playing on the Christian radio station and I prayed to God that we would find her phone before that song finished. When we took the turn and got back on the original trail, it was then that Jaime said, "I think I saw something." I thought, "no way." So I stopped. After all, the song was still playing, even though it was coming to an end. So she got off the bike and walked back about a city block and then I saw her holding up two items, for the phone had come apart, but nevertheless, it still worked. I told her that I had prayed, and she heard the tail end of the song... "God is in Control" by Twila Paris, I took a picture of her showing me the photos that she said she didn't want to lose, and I could see why. They were of her and her son, among many others.

We hit the road, trying to find our way back to her place and the next song was even better. I don't recall it specifically, but it had only one verse which was sung over and over again about how much our God Loves Us. It brought tears to my eyes and I knew God was telling my daughter just how much He loved her. I hope it was this moment that she renewed her faith in God and Jesus fully in her heart with no doubt. Now you know how God, our Searchlight, is also our Cell Phone Finder.

While many miracles occur while fully awake, sometimes, "dreams" are a reality...

Casual Miracle #8

Build It!

𝕭ave you ever been in that dream-like state which is not a dream, but offers clarity and/or comfort? I captured a vision, or visit as I like to call them, last night while I was lying in bed. I quickly arose and wrote it in my diary. **"Build It"** was what I saw—clear as day. More real than a dream. I was awake, but my eyes were shut. I had to ask myself, "Am I dreaming?" "Am I asleep?" But knew I wasn't. I knew I was awake. I had been sleeping, but I was awakened by a soft stroking on my right arm. I could feel it from my shoulder down to my elbow. Several times. It was real. I thought it must be my spouse, but I hadn't heard the bedroom door open. Then I got a little scared that someone else was in my room. The stroking happened again as if to reassure me that everything was alright. And then the vision came.

My eyes stayed closed and a 3D image of Lincoln log style pipes filled an area. I wondered "why?" They were in color and they seemed to be floating in the air in a 3D array. As I watched, the array quickly filled in with more and more of similar-sized "pipes." Until nearly the entire "room" or space had been filled. I tried to make sense of this but could not. I even asked, "what is?" and "why?" only to have the entire process repeat. This happened 3 times.

To be sure I was alone, I briefly opened my eyes to see the bedroom just as it was when I went to bed; the door shut, the lights dim. I then quickly took my left arm over to feel if my spouse had come up. She was not there. I tried then to reconstruct what had just happened. And I do think the vision did repeat itself several more times. Perhaps more by way of memory than revelation. It was only after meditation the next morning and after calming did the answer come. The stroking was, I believe, from an Angel reassuring me and comforting me while the vision was symbolic of building something.

What I eventually got out of this was *God* telling me to put pen to paper and **"build" this (His) book!** Which is nothing less than a casual miracle of its own. I have no doubt, after completing it that this very book you are reading took a casual miracle to write, edit, produce, print, market and get into *your* very hands. You—my dear reader—are part of this miracle! YOU are the culmination, aka, the end of this specific *casual miracle*. Consider yourself touched.

A few months later, I was alone in my room, lying in bed under my comforter, with my eyes shut and something grabbed both of my feet. Sure, this was an eerie experience but what I took from it was an angelic experience that I was supposed to get moving on this book. A few months later, it happened again.

Speaking of sleeping, sometimes God tells me just to "sleep on it" ...

Casual Miracle #9

Vacuum Cleaner

One day in Autumn, my vacuum bit it. I mean, I fried the motor but good. Not only was it clogged in all the hoses, but everywhere in between. The roller to the high-efficiency air outlet was jam-packed full. It was my fault really for not cleaning it out before taking on a heavy-duty project. I even heard and smelled the motor giving up the ghost so to speak. It was toast. Before totally giving up, I thought I'd tear into it and clean it as best I could. I had it all apart and even tried cooling off the motor. I mean it was HOT. I used the blower attachment of my shop vac to aid in cooling it down. The saying, "Let go and let God" entered my thoughts. So, I just left it overnight.

The next evening, I put it all back together and laid hands on it along with a prayer. I asked God if He would be my vacuum cleaner technician. I knew it would take a "casual miracle" to save this vacuum cleaner. With that, along with all the faith I could muster, I plugged it in and thanked God for making it come on -- and hit the power switch.

It was like it was brand new again. Like nothing I did the previous day did any damage whatsoever. Thanking God once again, I resumed vacuuming that heavy project and yes, pulled up a massive amount of dirt and grime that I had no idea was in that carpet.

How amazing is our God? The little bit 'o faith I could muster and the amount of thanking Him before seems so minuscule on a human level to me. But I know He loves me so much and I love Him so much. He just keeps on blessing me on a daily basis and on a personal level. Does He need the credit I continually give Him? I doubt it, but it certainly doesn't hurt. And among other things, He is now my vacuum-cleaner repair person.

Sometimes, it takes more than a *little* bit 'o faith...

Casual Miracle # 10

God is 'Our' Fireman

My friends and I were invited to shoot off some fireworks on a farm at our friend's house way outside of the city limits during the dry month of July. Now this place is a lot further out than I thought it was, but Idaho is still part of the wild west, so it should not surprise me when I have to travel some distance to get anywhere. After all the fireworks came out alarm bells were going off in my head as my inquiries as to safety measures seemed to go unheeded. "Oh well," I thought, "I hope they know what they're doing". So, I relaxed, sat back, and watched the show. All the way up until the "$175 massive box" containing who knows how many explosives inside was set on the gravel driveway, dry hay and straw bordering us on all sides, an old boat, the house; along with everything else you can imagine on a farm dating back to the 1950s. Everything but a hose. Yep, you guessed it. That one firework didn't perform as expected and suddenly there was *rocket's red glare* shooting all over the place starting fires all around us and a mere few feet from everything I just mentioned.

Everyone was running around looking for anything that would hold water; up to and including trying to get the well-water pump to deliver water all in order to douse the flames which should have burned the entire place to the ground. But miraculously, God took over and extinguished them all.

After what seemed like hours of stomping, running around looking for anything that would put out a fire, including a small kitchen fire-extinguisher, we examined the firework itself. Someone or perhaps, some **God** had extinguished over two-thirds of what could have, if all had gone off, been a complete disaster.

If that would have been considered a *hot* mess, the following would be considered a *cold* mess...

Casual Miracle #11

Ski Slope

My daughter, Hannah, and I enjoy snow skiing. After a perfect day of skiing with fresh powder - up to our waist powder - we boasted how neither one of us had fallen that day. So, it was on that final run that we really poured it on. Well, be careful of what you brag about because that invariably will cause the opposite to happen. We both went down, and I mean **hard!** After laughing it up, I realized one of my skis had left the area. There's a lesson here for those of you who have never partaken. Without both skis on your boots in three feet of powder, you have no way of staying up. You simply sink until you hit the hard-packed snow. Now here's where the problem manifests itself.

It turns out that it was the last run of the day. All the employees had "swept" the mountain and gone home. The only problem was, they didn't check the run we were on. In addition to that, the Sun was setting, my cell phone was dead

and hers was nearly dead. Even if our phones were charged, we had poor cell-phone service on the backside of this mountain. Add to that, it was Christmas Eve and the slopes were not going to be open the next day. See where this is heading? We were at least a mile from any civilization, and this was Bear Country and no way to get down the hill.
Enter God.

Since the employees and ski patrol all went home leaving us at the mercy of the elements, I prayed. Amidst the thoughts of bears and mountain lions joining us that night, I prayed for God to do His thing. I had no clue what that thing might be, for we were stranded up alone on a mountain that was getting darker and colder by the minute. Yet, I was at peace. God was already at work. I was also warm. Even though I knew there was no way of finding my lost ski and skiing down the mountain with my daughter to our car, I knew God was in the midst of us. And then the miracle happened. My daughter got a signal and called 911! Help was coming. She'd warmed her cellphone under her armpit and miraculously made one more call.

"We're stranded at Kelly Canyon on the far side." "We're sending help, just stay warm," was the response. And man did help come. It seemed an army of ski patrol, sleds, groomers, all came. They turned on all the mercury vapor lights until they found us a mile up the backside of the mountain and with apologies galore, they made us feel like we owned the place. I never did get my ski back, but no matter.

Some casual miracles are more profound than others, and some are downright phenomenal...

Casual Miracle #12

River Baptism

When seeking a sign as a Christian as to whether or not to pursue a certain course of action, oftentimes we will pray to God via Jesus. Sometimes the importance is so significant that the answer has nothing to do with this planet, so the answer must come from the element of the Trinity. Yes, I have been moved by the Holy Spirit before in my lifetime. And yes, I believe Angels have watched over me and helped me out of situations probably more times than I know. God will use whatever means He deems necessary to communicate with me in a way that is irrefutable and in a way that He knows I will accept. He knows me better than I even know myself. This instance could not be from any other source. And it is irrefutable. I cannot explain it away, nor do I need to explain it to anyone else. No one can take it away from me. I know what happened and it happened in a very personal way that only God knows would work with me. It is something I could not have shared at the time. So I am sharing it now... You'll only have to go on my ability to recreate this one precious minute in my life. The timeliness of which can only be from God. Because the timing, along with the song being played, was perfection. And He knew it.

One summer afternoon, my wife and I decided to attend a river baptism revival. We had both been praying about taking this step and while she was committed, I was yet to be convinced.

The following best describes what happened during, how I felt then, and how I feel afterward.

When Jesus appears before you, suddenly biblical names of chapters and verses and time have no relevance in His sight. They may mean little to you once Jesus appears and possibly even after the experience. For you will come to understand how they will always just be markings in a book for man's understanding. Jesus is a very personal Lord. What you see and know is real, no one else would see. So, cherish the moment. When it happened to me, I selfishly kept the experience to myself. For I knew that if I tried to share it, it would be gone. Besides, I was frozen. Some might say I was frozen by the Spirit. I could not talk. I did not try. But I felt my throat tighten. And I felt taller than usual. The experience set me apart from the crowd. Yes, I heard the music, the singers, the praise, but I was set apart from it. I was somewhat lifted up and perhaps maybe even a little shifted into another plane of existence. One where time did not exist. This is something you can't just casually say to someone. Like, "Hey, I just saw Jesus." Or, "Hey, Jesus just appeared before me." No, you leave this plane of existence just a little. As if there really are multiverses and you just experienced a bit of a shift out of this one. And, despite the festivities of the day, you don't really come back and fit in for a while. You almost feel like no one can quite see you. They almost seem to see *through you.* That's how I felt for the next few hours. So anyway, I held onto this information until I felt the need to share with someone I trusted and who just might understand what I had experienced — my Pastor.

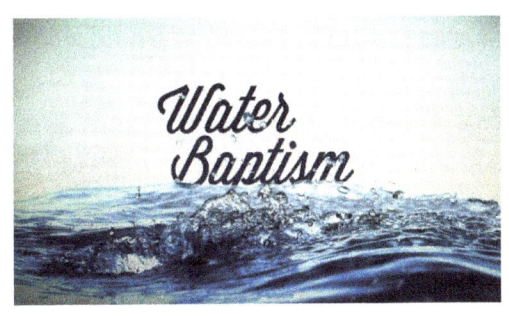

That is exactly what I did. A couple of hours after the experience and just before entering the river to be baptized as an adult, I whispered into my Pastor's ear that I had prayed for a week prior for a sign that I should do this, and I just received my sign. My answer. From the only one who could give me the only true, irrefutable sign. It shouldn't have surprised me that my Pastor's facial countenance didn't change one bit. His smile remained and his rhetoric simply added one phrase which was different from what he had been saying to all those others being baptized that morning... That I had received a *special anointing*.

And that was it. No words from Heaven saying, "This is my Son with whom I am well pleased". I guess those words were reserved for Jesus when He was baptized. And I felt no different after arising from the cool river water. Just wet and sandy. But I did it. And I may not have gone through with it had I not been given the sign I was looking for. Adult baptism is simply a proclamation of faith as an adult. It is a time in your life when you say to God and Jesus that you have no doubt of their existence and that you are firmly rooted in their existence, through *faith*. Now, baptism is not a requirement for salvation per se – more a public declaration of faith and willingness to follow Jesus. This is an act occurring as an adult after repentance and acceptance of Jesus Christ into your life.

Who wouldn't want to be baptized as an adult?

Ah, but there's a catch. You simply cannot fake your way through it. You cannot fool the Almighty God. The God who created all your senses knows you. Everything you see, feel, smell, taste, and hear. If you do not genuinely believe that He exists, you're only going to get wet (and sandy). That's all. And, you cannot earn your way into Heaven. If you think you can then once you get there, you'll only hear Him say, "Depart from me, for I never knew you." Sure, He rewards you according to the works you have done in bringing people to Him. But do NOT confuse that with doing works to earn your way into Heaven.

Ephesians 2:8-9 *For it is by grace you have been saved, through faith - and this is not from yourselves, it is the gift of God - not by works, so that no one can boast.*

 *Your Grace Is Enough* by Matt Maher

There is only one way to enter the kingdom of Heaven and that is through believing in the death and resurrection of Jesus Christ. You must come to Him first, in faith, then be baptized (which is optional), and then, when you leave this Earthly plane of existence, you will be welcomed into eternal life with Him in Heaven. In essence, you never die. It really is that simple.

Read more about this amazing experience in Part III...

Part II

More Casual Miracles & A Dream

𝕴n this section, I introduce even more casual miracles. In order to ensure the presence of God and casual miracles in *your* daily life, I feel it's important that you have a structure from which to build a continual prayer life. That is why, in addition to the "Sinners Prayer" you'll read in the last section of this book, I have included a couple of prayers you could use on a daily basis. And they go something like this. Additionally, I cannot think of a more fitting song than this:

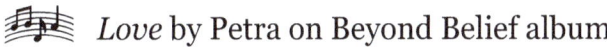   *Love* by Petra on Beyond Belief album

Pray and feel the peace our Father in Heaven instantly gives you. Begin by praising Him... as in *Our Father, who art in Heaven, hallowed be Thy Name.* Then *Pray* thanking Him for hearing you. *Pray* for humility. *Pray* thanking Him for forgiving you for all your sins. *Pray* for each and every member of your family, addressing key issues affecting each person specifically. And mostly, *Pray* for God's hand of protection on each of them. This is how you protect them. Your Spouse. Your Children. Your Grandchildren. Your Relatives. Even your friends and those whose petitions have come to your attention via prayer lists, social media, et cetera. Be specific. Take the time. Then, take all *your* cares to Him. Letting go of them and resting assured that He, *who loves you more than you can fathom*, will relieve you of all your worries. *Thank God* for sending His Son, Jesus, who died in place of you for giving you everlasting life, with Him. *Ponder* on this for a moment... Then, *thank God* for the faith He instills in you and for protecting you throughout the coming day. Finally, *thank* Him for all this and more, in the powerful name of Jesus Christ, your Lord, and Savior. Amen.

Before each meal, say this simple prayer that my grandparents, Mom & Pop taught me:

> "Come Lord Jesus be our guest. And let these gifts to us be blessed. Amen".

And before you go to sleep each night, teach this one to your loved ones, including yourself:

> "Now I lay me down to sleep. I pray the Lord my soul to keep. If I should die before I wake, I pray the Lord my soul to take. If I should live for other days, I pray the Lord to guide my ways. Amen".

Miracles have been around since Biblical times in both the Old and the New Testaments. God made abundant use of miracles in giving Christianity a start in the world. And He did so not only with Jesus, but by His Angels and His Apostles. You can find many of these using reference books. Miracles continue to this day, otherwise, I wouldn't be writing this book. Neither would other books be written that document them. Perhaps you have experienced a miracle or two in your own life?

If so, I would love to hear about them. You can submit them via the contact information found in the front of this book.

The Simple Truth

𝕴 had a dream. A very powerful dream. I call it "The Simple Truth." When I went to write it all out, it just flowed into *the truth*. The *God is My Plumber* type of truth. It just flowed onto the paper revealing the reality of Jesus and God's plan and how it all became so simple to me and how others try to change it – God's plan of Salvation – or make it difficult when there is only one way. I'm not targeting any one specific group; I'm targeting any that contradict the Word of God. For a comprehensive list of all the groups that seem to get it wrong, I invite you to obtain a copy of, Walter Martin's best-selling book, *The Kingdom of the Cults*. On a side note, I read this book when I was in a cult for a brief moment of time (about two years) during my young, impressionable years. So, I'm familiar with them. Without further ado, here is my dream:

Jesus is real. Everything He did was real. He is the Son of God—who is God—who became man, died, and rose again.

This is the simple truth. I see this as the only answer.

So many people are like lost sheep, unable to find their path in life, wandering aimlessly seeking to fill the Jesus-shaped void in their lives.

People want excitement, thrills, love or they'll turn to alcohol, cigarettes, sex, even illegal street drugs to fill that void. The problem with these is that the "high" doesn't last, meaningless sex is unfulfilling and often leaves one feeling emptier than before, even love can be fleeting. Only the love of Jesus lasts forever.

In any case, relying on other individuals can set one up for a fall. Disappointment. Rejection. Many of us can't seem to find that special someone of whom Solomon writes about, which is a series of love poems, unique in the Bible in its celebration of human sexuality and the passionate love between a man and woman. (God's Plan).

Why do people fight the One Simple Truth and Solution?

Truth is truth. It is unchangeable. Some will even take "the simple truth" and try to change it. According to some, the *Simple Truth* is now – all of a sudden – all wrong! They call it apostate; which is defined as, much of what has been before is now wrong. Doesn't that strike you as odd? Out with the old, in with the new; or their version of the new, that is. As if, the one God Almighty, who is the same from eternity past to eternity future, somehow changed His mind. That should set off alarms in your mind causing you to run away and run away fast. Keep this in mind:

The Scripture says, "The word of the Lord endureth forever." (1 Peter 1:25)

What it sounds like is that someone did not like it the way it was, for whatever reason, like the truth didn't suit their agenda, so they waited until the perfect moment to step in and try to change it up. Granted, some profess to have received a "vision" to which I can only respond with this verse:

Beloved, do not believe every spirit, but test the spirits, whether they are of God; because many false prophets have gone out into the world. – 1 John 4:1 (NKJV)

These people try to convince their prospective members that what was before was all wrong by giving them just enough truth to keep them from running away. Then, they change it up a bit.

I the Lord do not change – (Malachi 3:6)

Second, they make enticing promises which are relevant to each individual cult.

Third, they may even threaten ex-communication, loss of family or status, should their members try to leave or not follow them.

What did Lucifer promise Eve in the garden of Eden? "Take a bite of this (forbidden) fruit and you shall be like God."

One of Satan's tactics is to get rid of the Cross. The symbol Christians use to remind us of what Christ did for us and is why we celebrate Easter. The world has tried doing this by replacing the Cross with bunnies and eggs and has nearly succeeded!

Remember, the Cross is where Jesus defeated death and is where the whole plan of Salvation comes together. No wonder Satan wants it removed from the Church. Satan's objective is to get Jesus out of the picture; rewrite the story of Salvation or get rid of it altogether.

🎵 *The Cross Has the Final Word* by the Newsboys, Michael Tait, Peter Furler

Next, these cults replace the Bible with *their* version of the truth. This is basically called brainwashing. They say, "now here's how it *really* works..." And sadly, people with little to no Christian background fall for it. Why? Because it all sounds – so – good. Despite their being in a cult, I still love them. Love the sinner, hate the sin.

Look up Revelation 22:18-19 in the Holy Bible if you don't think this is a problem. From an Earthy standpoint, having a belief in a religion is good. People are generally more personable, honest, and hard-working. However, believing in working hard, and doing a lot of good things, that is, "works" to get you to Heaven doesn't follow God's plan of salvation.

The Bible specifically states in many places, that it is by Grace you have been saved, through faith, not of works (Ephesians 2:8). There is absolutely *nothing* you can do on your part to earn your way into Heaven. **Nothing.** Otherwise, why did Jesus have to die on the Cross? Now do you understand why the Cross is so important?

I've seen many "leaders," who are typically millionaires and billionaires, many of whom are "religious," but are they really? Or, are they more interested in "gaining the whole world" than following the one true Christ? I would hate to be in most of their shoes when they come to the end of their short-life and they have to answer the question Jesus will undoubtedly ask, *who did you say I am?*

For what shall it profit a man if he shall gain the whole world, and lose his soul? – Mark 8:36

For what is a man profited, if he shall gain the whole world and lose his own soul? – Matthew 16:26

So, just who was Jesus? Was He merely a prophet as many cults portray him?

Jesus says: *Anyone who has seen me has seen the Father* – John 14:9

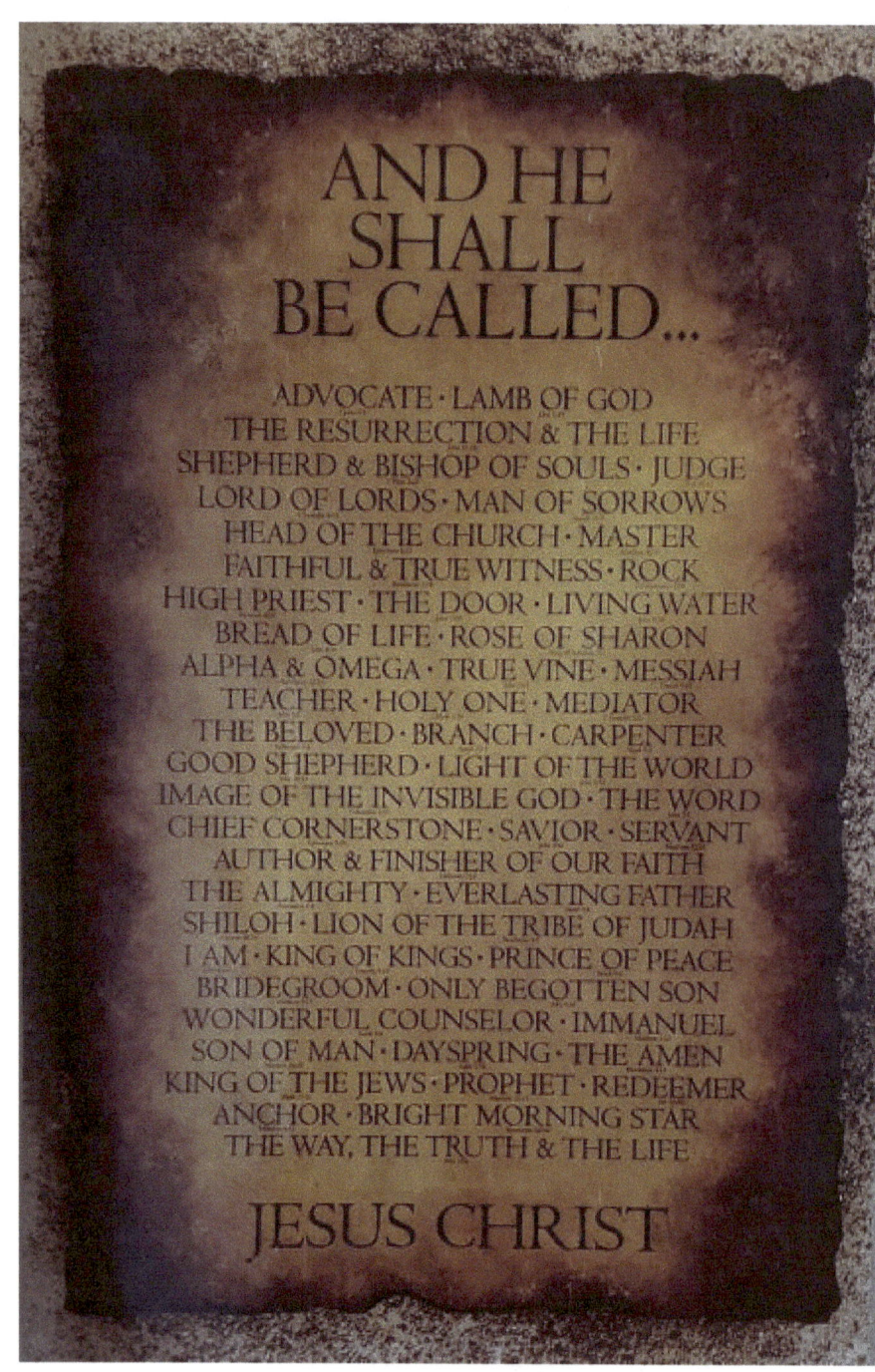

"I and the Father are one". – John 10:30

To summarize, people being people just need someone to follow and will oftentimes follow the one with the most charisma or enticements. Keep it simple. ***Just follow Jesus.*** Don't be tempted by false prophets and empty promises. Satan's sole purpose is to keep as many as possible from following *the truth. That's his sole agenda and he does it well.*

Having the gift of discernment, i.e., testing the Spirits, the reason why I don't sense the Holy Spirit in some people is due to the fact that they are not familiar with the truth. They are not filled with the Holy Spirit. One of my Spiritual Gifts (see Part VI) is being able to tell whether or not someone has a personal relationship with our Savior. And many in these cults do not. Am I saying that "they" never get filled with the Holy Spirit? No. Some do. If they profess Jesus Christ as their personal Lord & Savior who died on the Cross in place of them and rose again, acknowledging that He is the only way to make it to Heaven. It is all so simple. Don't mess with the truth. **His death on the Cross is the <u>only</u> way.**

John 14:6 - "I am the Way and the Truth and the Life. No one comes to the Father except by me."

Remember, we're still dealing with my dream here. Funny, "they" are not going to like it when I tell them this all came to me in a dream. Wait, haven't some of them received their "divine revelation" in a dream? Perhaps I should start a church too since God chose me with whom to share His revelation. I mean, what's the difference? For I have also had a revelation from the Almighty Himself. Seriously, I have. And you know what? It's no different than what the Bible already says. He hasn't changed a thing. *He didn't get it wrong!!!* So just save yourself some time and guilt and follow that, not me. So why me? And why this dream?

First, I think God knows I seek the truth. He also knows that I love and trust Him beyond a shadow of a doubt and will believe whatever He tells me. When God speaks, I listen. I think He appreciates that. I don't balk. I don't say, *"But God..."* I don't. I trust God implicitly. 100%. All the time. No second-guessing. I am the student; He is the Teacher. Whatever He says, goes. And because of this willingness to accept, and to listen, and to love Him, I feel that He blesses me by answering my prayers, according to His will, and communicates with me in a way that I know it is He doing the communicating. He doesn't really, that I can tell anyway, tell me to write it all down each time. I think He knows that I will anyway. God uses me as a vessel to help get His word out. And I trust that if I do write it down, He will use it if He wants to.

 *I Refuse* by Josh Wilson ... to sit idly by...

Now, that doesn't get me off the hook, so I don't have to do anything with it. But I do believe that He will open the doors, so these writings get to whomever He desires. Just as He preserved the Bible throughout the ages. No, I'm not saying that these are "holy scriptures" by any means whatsoever. Is revelation a Pastor gets from God and then passes onto the Church flock "Holy?" Maybe. But should it be treated as such? Well, maybe. But it's not. I believe God speaks to those who are willing to listen. *Let those who have ears hear* - Matthew 11:15. God is a very personal God. Does He use Angels to watch over us? Yes. There are many more accounts of Angelic sightings than I can keep track of. Remember, only a 3rd of the Angels turned on God and took off with Lucifer, who is also a created Angel. The other two-thirds stuck around and do God's bidding. And I believe they watch over us and protect us from harm. As an example, see Hebrews 13:1 - *Do not*

forget to entertain strangers, for by so doing some people have entertained angels without knowing it.

Who is it that whispers in your ear? What is your conscience? And what about the "high-pitched tone" of which you can't seem to pinpoint its source or timing? *For now, we see through a glass dimly, but then, face to face* - I Corinthians 13:12. We just cannot know and will not ever know until after we die and then we will know. But then, it is too late to come back and tell anyone. Your loved ones, your family, your friends... what is really on the other side. So, TELL THEM NOW!!! And the Holy Spirit will help you. Just plant the seed, and God's method will take over. You will be surprised. Those who you think are not savable, may just be.

At times, and when God desires it of me, I also have the gift of prophecy. I personally believe that everyone filled with the Holy Spirit can hear that "little voice" inside them, directing their actions and choices in life. Is that hearing the voice of God? I think that is a little different than hearing revelation. Some call that "little voice" your conscience. Does everyone have a conscience? Do powerful people who choose a life of crime have one? And if so, does everyone choose whether to listen to it or not? Whether you listen or not, I feel the "signal" or "volume level" gets louder or quieter. I personally feel that the more times you give in to that little voice, the more times it offers up advice. Why? Because it knows you will listen and heed. If you choose to continually ignore it, it diminishes. Sure, it never fully goes away, and thank God for that! So, you can conjure it up at any moment. And it is very willing to befriend you. Just like Jesus, who stands at the door and knocks. It is YOU, my dear friend, who must CHOOSE to open the door and invite Him in. That is a metaphor. What it means is, you must open up your heart and ask Jesus to come in. And you must do this with humility. Because YOU, my dear Sir or Ma'am were created by Him. For without Him, you would not BE. So put your ego aside just once and let Him in!

God does speak to me. Of course, everyone wants to know what He sounds like and those in the psychiatric profession want to know if I am "hearing voices". No. I am not. But I will tell you, it is like a best friend residing in my head. The thoughts come at a manageable pace. And the more I allow those thoughts to come, the more they do. Perhaps, because I am a willing subject, God has chosen to use me to communicate with His people. And that is everyone.

 *Make My Life A Prayer To You* by Keith Green

Yes, God did tell me, while I was in my teen years, that He was going to use me. He selected me and told me this because He already KNEW that I would be receptive. And why wouldn't I be? For no matter what life had planned for me, I ALWAYS knew that God was right there by my side. Whenever I needed or still need Him, I just call out to Him, in a sort of "prayer" (which is just talking to Him like He is your best friend), and He delivers me. I have never been in a fight. I have rarely ever been violated except when it was God's way of showing me or teaching me something. Do you want an example? Of course:

The Robbery

While in the Navy stationed in Norfolk, VA, I walked into a small convenience store in Virginia Beach, and it got robbed while I was there. Did I hear the voice of God? YES! Did I see the bullets bounce off the floor right in front of my face? YES.

Was I protected? I believe so. Would God let my macho Sailorism catch the guy? No. That wasn't part of the lesson. Well, actually, it was, if you think about it deep enough. So there. There's one of thousands of ways God has protected me and my family.

Stereo

Recall that I told you how this book got started by my kitchen sink unclogging itself in the middle of the night? Well, another casual miracle occurred just yesterday morning. I was upstairs getting ready for the day when I heard this LOUD & FRIGHTFUL noise coming from downstairs. As I descended the stairs, the noise got louder & louder. I thought, "what the heck is that noise!?" I didn't see anything, thank God, but I couldn't figure out where it was coming from. The vacuum cleaner was sitting next to the couch, but it wasn't on. So, what could it be? The noise was so loud that I had problems thinking. "JUST SHUT IT OFF!" my mind was screaming. But where, or what was it? Now, in a previous occupation, I'm trained to deduce emergency situations and respond in a timely manner, but this one was eluding me. It sounded like a lot of water. Then, I figured it out. The new Stereo Receiver I had tried to get working months ago, had come alive! It was still connected from when I was setting it up, but I could not get it to "wake-up". Well, apparently, God can. And did. There is absolutely no reason why it came out of latency on its own. It had been sitting there for months, next to my fireplace, which is also not working. The Receiver's volume was nearly all the way up and screaming "white noise" out of all six speakers to which it was hooked up.

Now, not only is God my plumber, but it seems that He is also my stereo repairman. I certainly hope that He likes fireplaces.

The Grandfather Clock

One Tuesday in Autumn, a friend came over and noticed I had an online auction on the computer. As I tarried in the kitchen, she casually mentioned that there was a grandfather clock on the auction. I hadn't noticed, so my interest peaked. After ten or twenty minutes had passed, I sat down at the computer and asked her about that grandfather clock. She remarked, "oh, I put it on the watch list." By doing so, it made it easier for me to access it and monitor the progress. How awesome. I said, "great, now I don't have to go searching for it."

As the countdown continued that afternoon, I watched and waited until there was under two minutes left on this week-long auction. I did not want anyone else to know of my interest in this particular clock. After researching the maker and upkeep requirements of this particular model, my anticipation rose. It's a pretty incredible find. Especially after having waited half a decade to find exactly what I was looking for. And it had to be special. It had to come to me in such a way, that I knew it was "the one."

I simply, and quietly asked God if it was alright to put another piece of furniture in this house, and patiently waited for His response. He said, "Can you afford it?" So, I went to look at my bank balance, and surprisingly, it was over a thousand dollars more than I thought I had. "Yeah," I told God (yea, right), and He said, "Go for it." So, I asked Him what amount should I bid? He responded, "$125."

As the auction counted down, I wanted to put a higher bid on it... you know, just in case God didn't know what He was talking about. But I didn't. I went and got a tall drink of water. I then watched as more bids came in, but none higher than mine. I then spoke some more with God... "You know God, winning this on a single bid could turn this house into a constant on the hour reminder of your love." The response I heard was "Be still and know that I am your God." I watched the clock tick down to the point where people will typically jump in, right at the last moment, to outbid you. But they didn't. As it counted down to 2 seconds, then one... I knew God was behind this whole thing.

Donating

So, what else? How does God continually bless me? He does so when I expect Him to and when I least expect him to. So, you see, I am not implying that I tell God Almighty what to do. He is just there for me because I am his willing servant. Take, for instance, the other day when I was approached by a Romanian in the parking lot of a store I was entering. As this guy showed me his 3x5 card with his message scrawled on it, *"I had already received the "ok" from God to donate"*. That is what I listen for in every instance before I give. God had told me several weeks prior to not touch that $20 bill in my wallet. I could have bought a pizza or any number of things with it. But every time I tried; God repeated his suggestion; *Don't use that $20*. When the Romanian man approached me, I instantly knew why. God had intentions for that bill. And I was thrilled beyond measure to give it to him. It says in God's Word, *He that giveth unto the poor shall not lack* – Proverbs

28:27. And yes, that was my Bible passage the very next morning.

God is my Real Estate Agent

My life has not always been easy. I have had trials and tribulations as I'm sure all of you have had. One of the biggest one is a devasting divorce. However, I have never been homeless. For after my divorce in Idaho, it was God who persuaded my brother to take me in and nurse me back to health. I have nothing but love, respect, and admiration for him for helping me through those trials and getting me back on my feet. And once I did, the moves were necessary in order to get back to my family and make things whole again.

While living with my brother and his family in Utah, I had a great job as an extra-board operator for a bus company. This kept my mind occupied as there were over one-hundred different routes a newbie had to learn and drive every day of the week. During this time, I sprouted my wings and moved into a studio apartment near the bus terminal. After nearly three years I felt it was time to make a change and go back home to Idaho, which is where my girls were.

🎵 *The Motions* by Matthew West

This was followed by a spontaneous 200 mile move that was nothing shy of a casual miracle, for, due to giving notice at work and my lease expiring, I had to move immediately. Pulling a U-Haul trailer with all my belongings and nowhere to stay, God led me to a newspaper ad from which I found a perfect 3-bedroom apartment; a place where I lived for five years. Never have I wanted for shelter in my life. From childbirth to now, my God has always provided for both mine and my family's needs. And for that, I remain humble and grateful. For God is a loving God for those who love Him. *We love Him, because He first love us.* – 1 John 4:19 (KJV)

After living in the rental which God provided me, I was ready to buy a house. That evening, God told me to drive a different route than I normally do. What is amazing is, the owner of the house I found had just nailed a *For Sale by Owner* sign to the tree in the yard. We met the very next day and the house and price were precisely what I had in mind. No realtor was involved as everyone, including the bank and title company bent over backward to push the deal through.

After living in that house for about ten years, that wonderful, solid house is now home to one of my girls (daughter), her new husband, and their growing family. Isn't God amazing!

Overall, I believe it was God teaching me lessons all along the way. Life is not always easy. For if it were, we would not develop character. We can do all things through Christ who gives us His strength. But never doubt that He uses others to carry out His plans. Even Adam needed a helpmate and that is why God created Eve. For it is not good that Man should live alone. All that being said, my family is back to where God wants it. For *what God has joined together let no man put asunder (separate)* – Matthew 19:6. We may not understand His workings and it may be painful, but as long as we keep Him first, all things work together for those who love Him.

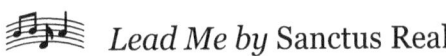 *Lead Me by* Sanctus Real

Asthma

In 1 Corinthians 12 and in Part VI of this book, you will read about the Spiritual Gifts. One of which is the Gift of Healing. I had always suspected that my faith being strong and my love for my family being as strong, especially during an emergency, that during a crisis situation I could call on God to be true to His Word. It was during one afternoon that we received a call from my Son-in-Law. He needed to know which emergency center to rush my daughter to as she was having a severe asthma attack and could not breathe! As you might have guessed... enter God! And thank God we live in a small town. After advising him as to the location of the nearest urgent care facility, I jumped in the car with 4-way flashers on and met them there. The doctors had already administered two vials of medicine, but they didn't seem to be working as my daughter was still having a severe panic attack and having trouble breathing. I immediately worked my way around to her back and laid hands on her and prayed for her healing. I could feel the power of the Holy Spirit move through me and into her and feel her calm. Of course, we had raised all of our children to love the Lord, so I knew she was a born-again Christian. That was never an issue. Dear readers, I implore you to raise up your children the same. Read them Bible stories before the world gets ahold of them. As it is written in Proverbs 22:6, *direct your children onto the right path, and when they are older, they will not leave it.* (NLT). I praise God to this day for the wellness and safety of all my children, grandchildren, and future great-grandchildren.

Ribs

Not long after the above true story about my daughter's asthma attack did a similar situation present itself with my wife. For weeks she had issues with broken ribs. What had happened was one morning she got out of bed and, as some of you pet lovers know, tripped over our beloved dog. She fell against the dresser and broke several ribs. Now there is not much you can do for broken ribs except let time do its thing. After several weeks had gone by with seaming little to no healing taking place, I thought, enough is enough. So, I laid hands on her ribs and asked God to heal them. And you guessed it, her complaining stopped almost immediately. It was either my faith or hers or a combination of both, but God delivered.

Some people have asked me why does it matter if I follow God and become a Christian? These last two testaments should give you cause. If everlasting life isn't reason enough.

> Disclaimer: The Spiritual Gift of Healing is one of the gifts of the Holy Spirit and is given to us for the purpose of service to others. Now please, don't misunderstand. I am not claiming to be some kind of miracle worker like those T.V. evangelists who draw a crowd and have people line up so they can lay hands on them and heal all their afflictions. So please, as much as I would like to heal everyone in the world, that is not my calling. All I know is that when you pray and apply enough faith, God can and will work wonders. I urge you to seek out your local Pastor for prayer if you need healing.

Our Annual Yard Cross

Easter is not about bunnies & eggs! It is our tradition to display a lighted Cross in our front yard, much like putting up a tree around Christmas time. Only this year we couldn't find the waterproof light used to illuminate the Cross. This light is as much needed as putting lights on a Christmas tree. After searching all the normal places one would store such an item, I had pretty much given up when I resorted to the last resource available to me: Prayer. Almost immediately after asking God to help me find the necessary light, I heard the proclamation, "FOUND IT!" from my wife. God does not waste any time.

Sunglasses

Remember how God was our Searchlight in *Casual Miracle #7*? Well, a similar incident occurred just yesterday and right before this book went to print involving the same motorcycle. We went on a 45-mile ride to get our favorite huckleberry ice cream cone in Swan Valley, Idaho. It was a beautiful day for a ride—no jacket required; however, upon our return trip, out of nowhere came a ferocious side-wind which required me to hang onto the handlebars with both hands! My passenger tapped on my back and I thought it was because she saw my sunglasses blow off my face. What had happened was, *her* sunglasses had also blown off *her* face. So, I pulled off the road and we retraced our path all the while I was praying for God to produce yet another casual miracle. We had been travelling 65 miles an hour, so we had a lot of ground to cover. It's helpful to not worry, have little doubt and a whole lot of faith when praying to God. I don't know if I had more faith than Lisa because, on the side of the road were my fairly new (and very expensive) prescription sunglasses. Sorry to say, she never found hers. The positive aspect though is that her glasses were three years old and she needed a new pair anyway. However, the casual miracle doesn't end there! God takes care of His children; as I went in to have my scratched lenses replaced... for free.

We waited a few days before calling our eye doctor and wouldn't you know it, they were closed. Here's where the miracle came. Even though they were closed, an employee saw the flashing light on the phone and answered it. He said they were over a week out in getting new appointments, but he would check for any cancellations. After being on hold for a minute or so, he came back on and said someone cancelled just an hour ago and could we come in tomorrow! So not only is God our eyeglasses finder, but He is also our eye-appointment manager.

Worry versus Faith

Many times, we go along life's path worrying about this and worrying about that when it really isn't necessary. Here is why. **Worry is the opposite of Faith.** I mean think about it. If you are worried about something, then you have discounted that God can fix it. Do you think God is not big enough to solve your problem? Whatever it is? *For God hath not given us the spirit of fear; but of power, and of love, and of a sound mind* (KJV) – 2 Timothy 1:7. Have you forgotten that God created the entire Universe? And that God oftentimes sends his Angels to intervene on His behalf. See Part V for three books that you can read regarding many stories of Angelic encounters.

Worry might be brought about by dabbling in any one of the seven "deadly sins." They are gluttony, envy, lust, greed, pride, wrath, and slothfulness. One, especially, is wanting more than you have. We need to learn to be satisfied with what we have. There's a great jazz tune by Tom Scott entitled, "Greed." It goes something like this—

♫ *If it's more than you need... it's greed.* ♫

I guarantee that once you start writing down all the casual miracles God performs in your daily life, your worries will become less, and your faith, i.e., believing, will become stronger. Your walk with the Lord will become bolder as will your prayer life. You will find yourself "talking" more with God as though He was right there with you all the time. You know why? Because He is. Life really is better with Jesus.

🎵 *Grace Got You* by MercyMe "Smile, like you just got away with something..."

Here are some verses regarding putting your trust in the Lord:

Trust in the Lord with all your heart and lean not unto your own understanding; but in all your ways acknowledge Him, and He will make your paths straight. Proverbs 3:5-6.

This one verse sums it up nicely. There is so much that I don't understand. It's so refreshing that I don't have to. I just need to let go and let God, and He will direct my path. Isn't that wonderful? What a friend we have in Jesus. How's the song go?

What a friend we have in Jesus
All our sins and griefs to bear
And what a privilege to carry
Everything to God in prayer

Oh, what peace we often forfeit
Oh, what needless pain we bear
All because we do not carry
Everything to God in prayer

Have we trials and temptations?
Is there trouble anywhere?
We should never be discouraged
Take it to the Lord in prayer

Can we find a friend so faithful?
Who will all our sorrows share?
Jesus knows our every weakness
Take it to the Lord in prayer

~Written by Joseph Scriven~

What a Friend we have in Jesus by Alan Jackson

Do not be anxious about anything, but in every situation, by prayer and petition, with thanksgiving, present your request to God. – Philippians 4:6

Therefore, I tell you, do not worry about your life, what you will eat or drink, or about your body, what you will wear. Is not life more than food, and the body more than clothes? – Matthew 6:25

Look at the birds of the air; they do not sow or reap or store away in barns, and yet your heavenly Father feeds them. Are you not much more valuable than they? – Matthew 6:26

Can anyone of you by worrying add a single hour to your life? – Matthew 6:27

Therefore, do not worry about tomorrow, for tomorrow will worry about itself. Each day has enough trouble of its own. – Matthew 6:34

Cast all your anxiety on Him because He cares for you. – 1 Peter 5:7

Part III

More Casual Miracles

River Baptism Miracle continued...
Expanded Jesus sighting section!

$\mathcal{N}$ow that I had seen Jesus and since He devoted Himself to me for about a solid minute, my week-long prayer was answered. The image above is the best representation I've found of His face. On a side note, did He have to leave everyone else and the entire world for that minute to appear before me? I know that's a silly question. About as silly as, why couldn't anyone else there see Him? And, why couldn't I speak and say anything to anyone, *Hey! There's Jesus! Right There! Right in front of me! Can't You See Him???* Isn't God remarkable? Not only could I not speak, but I felt like I was just a little above and to the left of this Universe. Just by a few inches, where time didn't exist. Like, one foot was in and one was out. Of course, this is one of those, 'you have to experience it for yourself before you can fully appreciate it' moments. It's like trying to describe what cold water feels like to someone who has no idea what water is, much less this concept of "cold." Until you jump in, you won't really know. And then try to describe it to someone else who has never felt water before. Anyway, I know what I experienced did happen. Jesus hung around until He knew all my doubt disappeared. And I'm a fairly complex individual, having a degree in subatomic nuclear particles, with a minor in Philosophy and pretty much life in general. I looked away once to test my vision (among other things) and then slowly looked back, just to give time enough to cause whatever was happening to go away. It didn't. His **face** was still there.

Then I drank it in. As you can imagine. I etched it in my memory banks and did not even want to test the previous theory again. I watched and watched and watched and listened to the Church's choir praising God with a specific song that I attached to that memory. I smelled the air and attached that to His face. I felt the wind and what little I could of the grass below my feet. I wore sandals that day but was standing barefoot on the park's grass. I attached all my senses to that moment to help ingrain His visage permanently into both my short and long-term memory banks. At the time of writing this, it's been three days since my baptism, and I can still conjure up the entire episode like it just happened.

I feel so much joy, and love, and peace knowing that God loved me enough to show Himself to me. How many people actually have this happen to them? Many people think that they are due this communication from God. Like, it's God's job to report to them. Ha! What a joke. I think that I humbled myself sufficiently in the eyes of our Lord that He gave me a gift. A "special anointing" if you will. The only gift a person could ever really want while living their life. My prayer for the week before was asking God if He wanted me to be baptized in the river that day. And if He did, I prayed that He would show me a sign. One that would be irrefutable and that I would know beyond a doubt that it was He who sent the sign. I'd say He did.

Now my point was that, since Jesus' appearance to me, if my faith had waivered before, it does not anymore. I am all in. 100%. I have absolutely no doubt of any of this Christianity stuff. Now, I know this book is all about the little "miracles" that happen in many lives, including my own, and that, in itself, should be enough to prove His existence. But with this latest miracle, I now know, beyond a shadow of a doubt, that God is real. Jesus is real. The Holy Spirit is real. The Bible is real, and everything in it is real. I simply cannot get enough reading, hearing or listening to Christian music. I'm immersed in it all the time now. And, I'm at peace now when I didn't used to be. Things that used to bother me for no reason, do not anymore. God takes care of His followers, His sheep. And I know that He is taking care of me. I have nothing to worry about. And all He asks of me is to tell others about Him.

Now, that is so easy to do. I see people now through the eyes of love. I love everyone now. It doesn't matter who you are or what you have done. I simply love you. And that makes it so easy to give the credit to the source of love, Jesus. There are two commandments Jesus left us with. The first is to love the Lord your God with all your heart, and with all your soul, and with all your mind. And the second is like the first, and that is to love your neighbor as yourself. – Matthew 22:36-39. And who doesn't love themselves? We all do. Until Satan tries to fool us into thinking we are no good. So as believers, you have the power to cast Satan and his minions aside by invoking the name of Jesus. They have no choice but to flee. Once you do this, then see how you feel about yourself. You love yourself. And you are to love others that way, too. As a matter of fact, God has equipped us to love others. I've found that by writing this book and using the word "love" over 72 times has made it easier for me to love. Try it. Try writing down how much you love other people and see for yourself how much easier it gets. There's even a song playing on KLOVE that helps:

 Love God Love People by Danny Gokey

God Created the Law of Attraction

While the world's view of the law of attraction is rooted in secular thinking, it originated from God Himself. Just like the law of gravity, the Almighty spoke it into being when He was creating the Universe. What do you think Jesus meant when He said, "Ask, and it shall be given you; seek, and ye shall find; knock, and it shall be opened unto you." Matthew 7:7 – Or, as Paul stated in his letter to the Galatians, "Be not deceived; God is not mocked: for whatsoever a man soweth, that he shall also reap." Galatians 6:7.

"I Am" statements emerged from "The Law of Attraction" also known as "The Secret". These are positive statements you make about yourself in order to make them come true. The problem with making such a list is that it is not exhaustive. What if you leave something out?

Being "chosen" so to speak, God has elected to continuously bless me. And, like I've said, once you start keeping track and documenting your blessings, the more will come and at a faster rate! Who would not want that, you ask? Well, a man's gotta sleep. I am not immortal... yet. I caution you to not confuse lists such as morning affirmations or "I Am" statements with the unmistakable miracles of which this book is about. These may seem like coincidences but have no other explanations as to why they occurred. You must simply *give God the credit*. His timing is always perfect. Always. Maybe He does this so He gets the credit. When He answers your prayer – at the very last instant – when all other avenues have been exhausted, you simply *know* and must give Him the credit.

Thoreau is given the credit for the quote: "If you advance confidently, in the direction of your dream, and endeavor to live the life you have imagined, you will meet with a success, unexpected, in common hour." Well, he may get the credit for the quote, but God gets the credit for the why and the how and the hope!

> *But those who hope in the Lord will renew their strength. They will soar on the wings like Eagles; they will run and not grow weary; they will walk and not be faint.* — Isaiah 40:31

🎵 *You Keep Hope Alive* by Mandisa, Jon Reddick

That being said, God is my "solution" to every problem. And it remains that the peace I feel at times is Him residing in me... "that is beyond all understanding." – Philippians 4:7 Amen. For you, I'd just say, Pray. For every prayer is answered. Just remember one thing. It may not be in the way you think you wanted it to be answered. For God sees your heart. And, God sees the future. He knows where you will be in ten, twenty, or fifty years. And the answer to that prayer may come five decades later. And you will probably be the wiser because of it.

So, I keep coming back to the main point that I want you to understand. God speaks to me. And I chose to start capturing the miracles as they occurred in my life. The first one I chose to capture was when He, God, by whatever resource He uses, His Angels probably, unclogged my kitchen drain. I was so blown away by that. I KNEW that it was God's intervention, and so I started this book. Hence, the name, "God is My Plumber, and Other Casual Miracles". Once you start giving God the credit for the little things, (and they are ALL little things to Him—after all, He did create the entire Universe), He'll start making more things happen.

Now, I don't wish to come across as presumptuous here, as though I know what God thinks and feels; however, according to Scripture, we know that it is good and right to praise Him. So, it is natural to assume that He also wants the credit when He causes these casual miracles to happen. Afterall, that is just another way to spread His message to others through you. Does God have an ego? No. (He doesn't care what you call Him, as long as you call Him.) And I also believe it pleases

Him to reward those who do acknowledge Him. He is a very giving God. After all, He gave His only begotten Son to die on the Cross!! I would never do that... give up my son to get tortured and crucified. But God did. So yeah, I'd say God is a giving, loving God, who sent His one and only Son to die IN YOUR PLACE, on that tree on Calvary some two thousand years ago. Now *you* don't have to die an eternal death. Hallelujah! All you are asked, and reasonably so, is to accept the fact that Jesus took your place. Is that too much to ask?

Remember when we were stranded on the ski hill on Christmas Eve with no cell phone service? God was only a prayer away. God doesn't rely on Verizon. He is the most <u>reliable</u> wireless communication service. And He protects and delivers. God is our 911 and our 411. We love Him and go to Him first because He first loved us. Why would anyone not subscribe to Him? Besides, He's free. All He asks for is your complete and undivided loyalty.

And last, but never the least...

God is my muse and encourages me to write. It was He who set me on my mission in my teenage years. It's been He who has kept me safe all my life. Biblically, it is put this way... *He who began a good work in 'you' will be faithful to complete it.* – Philippians 1:6 That is a statement that not only exists in His Word, the Bible, but I feel it in my mind, body, heart, and soul. I have no doubt that He will be faithful "to complete it." Sometimes, I would just like to know when! But that is just me getting in my own way. By nature, I am impatient. "Just keep writing Mike." And so, I do.

Part IV

Casual Miracles as Told to me by Others

I'm not the only one who experiences casual miracles. Perhaps you do too? For instance, here are a few casual miracles shared with me. God or their guardian angels were definitely with them.

Tim Tebow and "John 3:16"

The God that we serve is such a "Big God." Want Proof? Do an Internet search on Tim Tebow's John 3:16 story.

In essence, Tim Tebow, a football player, had written John 3:16 under his eyes. Three years had now passed and his friend told him, in his recent football game that he had passed for 316 yards, averaging 31.6 yards per pass, yards per rush was 31.6 and the CBS rating peaked at 31.6.

A lot of people would say it's a 'coincidence', but Tim Tebow simply said, "Big God."

Lisa's Casual Miracle

"During my teenage years, I was very involved with my church's youth group and every year we would go on a winter retreat up to a parishioner's cabin in the mountains. It was a wonderful weekend filled with worship, cross-country skiing, and hot cocoa.

Our pastor, Father Bob, always had to leave on Saturday evening in order to conduct services back in town on Sunday. This particular year, I was scheduled to be the lay reader on Sunday morning, so I rode back with Father Bob Saturday night.

Let me tell you a little about Father Bob – he was a rather imposing figure standing well over 6' tall with a resounding voice, perfect for preaching the Word. Yet, he was the most gentle, personable, and fun minister I had ever know. In fact, in spite of his lengthy frame, he drove a little two-seater Triumph TR7 sports car.

We were in this car on our way back down the mountain when we encountered a blizzard. The roads turned to sheer ice. Father Bob was driving carefully, but nothing could have prevented what happened next. While we were crossing a bridge over the river (some 100' down), we began to spin out. That little car plunged headlong toward the side rail, destined for the river below. It was imminent death.

Then came the miracle. It was though the hand of God came down and gently stopped the car without as much as a jolt. Suddenly, we were just sitting there with the nose of the car barely touching the side rail. "Thank you, Jesus" was all I could say. I'm very grateful I was in such good company – meaning both Father Bob and the Lord."

Tire Blowout!

My daughter had a front tire blowout on her car while driving on the freeway and spun 360 degrees on highway 65 in the left lane crossing three lanes of traffic ending up on the shoulder. Either God or her guardian angel was definitely with her. Here is the story in her words...

"I have a fairly lengthy commute (about 40 minutes each way) and about half of that time is spent on the interstate. A couple years ago, I was headed to a late-morning work meeting (miracle #1 because there wasn't the usual Nashville rush hour traffic), going 70 MPH, and my front-right tire blew. I had been driving in the far left lane and when the tire went, I spun to the right, all the way around while watching oncoming traffic headed straight for me, and ended up in a ditch on the right side of the highway. Still, to this day, I have no idea how my car didn't collide with another vehicle or the median. To add to the miraculous nature of this story, the ditch I landed in was relatively flat, unlike the side of the road in either direction that had steep hills and metal guard rails that would have caused serious damage. My car stayed on all four wheels, didn't flip, didn't hit anything at all, and I was physically unscathed. To top it all off, I didn't have to go to that meeting."

Luke 6:38

~Give, and it will be given to you~

My daughter, Tara, is blessed. She'll even admit it. Perhaps she says this because I've told her so. Goods things happen to her and her family. She has a wonderful husband, two beautiful daughters and a job she loves. She is also attending college *in her spare time*. They live in a great home which she finds time to plant gorgeous flowers and plants in and all around. I've wondered how it is that she *attracts* all this goodness to her life. When we were out shopping together just the other day is when her "little secret" was revealed.

You see, not only is she very thrifty but she also has a bubbly, magnetic personality; you can't help but smile when you are around her. After we were through shopping, she swiped her card in the self-checkout counter and the screen asked if we wanted to donate a dollar to some charity. Without thinking, I immediately pressed the "no" button (cause that's *my* default reaction to that question) and didn't think anything of it. My daughter just looked at me with a puzzled look and said, "Hey, why'd you do that? I was going to donate a dollar. I ALWAYS DONATE A DOLLAR. It doesn't matter where I'm at or what the cause is, I just always donate a dollar." Wow! I was blown away. That's her secret. And that's why she *attracts* so much goodness to her life! She's a giver. Now, and forevermore, whenever I'm presented with the option to donate, you can bet I'm pressing the dollar button.

Ethan's Daughter

"My beloved father passed away on the first of December. It was a difficult week off work. Planning a funeral, writing an obituary, preparing for a eulogy. I was able to attend a fitting with a prosthetic doctor who was fitting my daughter for a formative helmet. It was to be her fifth and final meeting before beginning to wear her new helmet. My father, the day before he was hospitalized, had asked how much the cost of the helmet. It was nearly $6,000. My father wrote a check on the spot for the full total.

We had been doing exercises with my daughter. Head massages; neck massages—which she detested and would scream and cry in pain throughout. With no noticeable effect to the measurements of her skull.

In the midst of meeting with funeral directors & well-wishers, I joined my wife, my 2 year old daughter, 4 year old son, and 7 month old baby girl, at the doctor's office. When the doctor examined her head, scratched *his* head, remeasured & explained how her cranial plates had shifted and how there would be no need to measure her for a corrective helmet. I believe that my father petitioned the Lord to help my daughter that day.

It was, with no doubt, a miracle."

Easy Ways to Add Casual Miracles to YOUR Life

Do you want casual miracles in your life too? Here are some simple ways in which you can start to make them happen:

I love the clarity I have in the morning. Even before my first cup of coffee, this is what dawned on me this particular morning.

We have an old wooden Cross hanging on the wall just outside our front door. I really love being reminded of what Christ did for me. Satan, however, thinks otherwise. Get this one right. Satan is the cause of all the hate, corruption, and wars that occur. Do not blame God. Don't say, "God, why did you let this [bad thing] happen to me!" God is Love. In mathematics, the word "is" is an equal sign, "=". Thus, God = Love. Read on.

Satan is the "author of confusion". He loves confusion. This is how he operates. The first thing Satan likes to do is get Jesus out of the picture. One way he does this is by removing the Cross from the walls of buildings. That's his main thing. Then, he'll try to tell you (confuse you) that all those truths you hold so dear, are false, or wrong. Then, he'll feed you full of misinformation. Anything but the correct truth. He'll mislead you away from God. Satan hates it when you follow the simple truth.

Are you under attack when you are on the wrong path? No. Are you when you read God's word? Oh ya. Majorly. People stay on the wrong path because their lives are so cushy. They are comfortable. Life is great. They are dreaming big and accomplishing goals. And they are teaching all this wonderful stuff. Satan is leaving them alone. Why? Because these people aren't following God! And that's the way Satan wants it.

Start following God via the Bible, and I bet you—initially—your life falls to pieces. Been there. Done that. This is not to say that all non-believers have it easy, nor that all Christians are miserable. God does prevail in the end. Revelation 11-15. Jesus came that we (Christians) might have life and have it more abundantly (John 10:10). My life is pretty amazing! God wants us to worship Him. We are His creation. He'll even try to get our attention should we start to ignore Him. He does this by lifting His hand of protection. (Read the story of Job, the 18th chapter in the Old Testament). Let me add this wonderful truth.

How do you talk to this most Holy God (who is Spirit, by the way – John 4:24)? Prayer. And by what mechanism do we use? Faith. Take the step in faith and God will then be there to catch you. That is how He operates. Christians, by definition, follow Christ. Especially the part where He took on all the sins of mankind. He did that and suffered horribly. More so than any of us endure during our brief existence on this planet. I can't thank Jesus enough for taking my place on that cross. Also, *by having the faith as small as a mustard seed, you can say to this mountain, move from here to there and it will move. Nothing will be impossible for you.* – Matthew 17:20

So, in summary, display a cross, (ours will remain on our wall as a constant reminder of His love and a witness of our faith), start following God's word by picking up the Bible, pray and in doing so, you might just find casual miracles increase in your life too.

Part V

Proof that the Bible is a Historical Document

𝕴 am going to relay to you indisputable proof that the Bible is what the Bible says it is and that it is not just some fictional book gathering dust on your bookshelf. And I am going to do this from many perspectives, starting with mine, and then leave with the experts in hopes that you will not have any place left to turn to refute the ***fact*** that the Bible is the Word from God who is the Creator and Master of *Everything*.

My Testimony

You ever look at a beautiful sunset and think, only God could have painted such a beautiful portrait in the sky. How about this one? Your children. Your newborn child. The first time you hold that precious little miracle... And all the while they are growing up doing and saying the cutest little things. What would you do without them? How many times have you prayed over them for their safety while they lay sleeping so innocently in their cribs or their beds and as they grow up?

 *Butterfly Kisses* by Bob Carlisle

Back to my life. I have never been in a fight. Why? You might ask. Or not... anyway, I attribute that to guardian angels. There were many times when I should have, but I managed to escape this animalistic method of 'working things out.' I could not even bring it on if I wanted to! "God, please let me kick someone's ass!" "No," He says. "Your strength comes from me, not from your fists".

Philippians 4:13 - *I can do all things through Christ who strengthens me.*

Why fight it?

It's not enough to just have God speaking to you in a way only you can discern, is it? This in itself should be proof of His existence. Even when instances occur on Earth which are predicted or mentioned in the Bible, you still use every trick in the book to avoid recognizing the truth.

For example, as of February 2015, in Sweden, they are implanting microchips in their hands for the convenience of "entering a building or using the company printer". This was foretold in the Bible. And I remember saying to myself that I would never have one of these. But humanity just accepts it without a passing thought. People! This was predicted in the

Bible! If you would just get outside of yourself for a moment, you would see that the Bible is real. That it all points to a Savior. One that would be born of a virgin woman, impregnated by the Holy Spirit. (No, not an alien). The same Spirit who visited the Apostles in the Upper Room after Jesus left the Earth. This Spirit put dancing flames on their heads to show they were filled with the Holy Spirit. That same Spirit you get when you repent of your sins, confess the reality of Jesus - who died on the Cross in your place, and rose again - and accept Him into your heart. In other words, accept that He is real, that God is real, and there is a whole world beyond what we see with our eyes, just waiting for us, through faith, to say "yes".

It is all pretty simple really. Everything I have just said is factual. As factual as splitting atoms or anything else science wants to take credit for. I believe all inspiration given to man for the sake of progress, is God-breathed. In His perfect timing, He gives original thoughts to specific people, who then carry out *His* "invention". Take any device... the telephone, the microwave, the computer, automobiles, airplanes, even modern medicine... you name it, and God invented it. If you would feel more comfortable saying that God made "man" smart enough to figure things out, then, fine. But God did create man with a brain that is intuitive with the ability to learn and draw conclusions. So, God still gets the credit.

It was through His original creation, that He put everything here that we would need to function as a people. The Sun, oil, natural gas, coal, magnetism, and even the ability to split atoms in a nuclear power plant are all ways for man to "create" energy. The flow of electricity through a wire, the signals coming from satellites to your television, yes, even the law of attraction, whereby you reap what you sow (biblical), is a creation of God.

Even our Founding Father, Thomas Paine said, *All the principles of science are of Divine origin. Man cannot make, or invent, or contrive principles; he can only discover them. And he ought to look through the discovery to the Author.*

Our infinite God, the one you simply cannot comprehend, because He knows you cannot fathom the truth until you die and go to Him, acknowledges *for now we see through a glass darkly, but then, face to face* (1 Corinthians 13:12). That *then* is when you die. All your misbeliefs will be shown to you. Unfortunately, it will be too late for you to tell anyone back home - here on Earth - the truth.

The Bible tells us everything we need to know. So why do people fight it? Simple. It has to do with the fact that the Devil is loose in this world. Lucifer challenged God. God prevailed. Lucifer got kicked out of Heaven and took a third of the angels with him. Now he is called Satan. He and his followers are simply upset and cause all the hate, destruction, and discontent on Earth. They will try to keep you from knowing the truth. They will hide your Bible (if you own one), make you not want to go to church, and do everything in their power to steer you from the one and only truth. What are some of the things they do? From divorcing a family unit to creating cults that are as far from the truth as you can possibly imagine. Anything they can do to manipulate your mind away from the only truth on this planet, the Bible.

But thank God we are stronger than Satan and his minions. *For greater is He that is in me, than he that is in the World.*

I John 4:4. And in order to have the "He" in you, you must be "born again".

Your first birth is when you entered into this world. That is when you are born the first time. You become "born again" when you accept Jesus (whose father is God... and who is God Himself... and who died a horrific death on the cross, so that you wouldn't have to), into your heart. And make Him your personal Lord and Savior.

Why is that so hard for you to do? Is it because of what your so-called friends might think? Is it because you are just so smart? Just remember, it was God who created that 'smart' brain of yours. So you had better be giving Him thanks for your "smartness". You've got it all figured out, don't you? You have dug up bones of prehistoric man and fossils of fish, and how about those dinosaurs? Surely all that evidence demands an explanation. With every turn of the trowel, science is now validating the Bible. See: www.IsGenesisHistory.com among other sites mentioned in Part V of this Book.

Fine. Go ahead and miss out on the favors from God. Don't recognize Him even for a second. Go get your Ph.D.'s. But don't come crying to me when you get to the end of your life and wonder where you are heading next! Also, what does the expression, "There are no atheists in foxholes" mean to you? Wouldn't it be more prudent to just give faith a chance?

There are answers to every question. You just have to expend a little energy exploring. Now that we have the internet, go ahead and search for biblical answers to all these questions. Do it on your own time, when no one else is looking. Go ahead, you have my permission. But just know one thing, the resistance you are feeling, that is the devil and his followers trying their best to keep you from the truth. Open your mind. Study. And let me know what you find out.

One great way to study is to join the "Proverbs of the Day" club. There are 31 Proverbs in the Bible, so you can gain wisdom by always having something to read. On the 1st day of the month, read Proverbs 1, on the 2nd, read Proverbs 2, and so on and so forth.

One thing that I have found out is that no demon can stop me from praying. You see, God gave us free-will. And with that, the ability to think. To have thoughts that you control. And you know what else? God can hear your thoughts. Yep. He can. So direct some of those thoughts into talking to Him. Simply talk to God like you would a good friend. He's got time. (Which doesn't exist for God... quite a mind-blow, huh?) He is as patient as your best friend... your dog. But even more than that. You see, God is Love. Pure, unadulterated Love. That's why He is so patient with you. He loves you. And believe me, you are worth loving. God thinks you are. And that really is all that matters.

 *No Hopeless Soul* by Stephen Stanley

Whether you are having a good day or a horrible day, God is always there, waiting, listening, ready. You can always go to Him in prayer (talking to Him in your mind... or out loud, your choice). And believe me when I say, you will always feel better after you do. How do I know? Decades of trusting in Him. That's on my résumé. That is the experience I bring to you today. Boy if you even knew. Man. The situations I have gotten myself into where there was simply no other way out. But I am still here!

🎵 *I Am Not Alone* by Kari Jobe

Speaking of "still being here," I never ever considered the alternative. You know what I mean. Even when times were tough, I've always put my family first and would never leave them by considering suicide. If you ever need help in this regard, you can reach out and talk to someone by calling: 1-800-282-8255 (TALK). If you've experienced the loss of a loved one, you'll find some emotional support by listening to this song:

🎵 *Scars in Heaven* by Casting Crowns

Personally, I believe God is using me right now. You think I am smart enough to write this book on my own? I don't think so. The words are merely flowing 'through me'. As a matter of fact, I believe this book is another *casual miracle*! I am a vessel being used by the almighty God. AND I LOVE IT. I take little credit for writing this. Except for that typing class I took way back in school. All levity aside, not only does God love you, but I love you as well. Granted, mine is Phileo love. While God's is called Agape love, otherwise known as unconditional love. There is absolutely nothing you can do to lose the love that He has for you. Well, almost nothing. He doesn't really appreciate Satan worshipers. But then, you'll have to take that up with Him, if you make it to Heaven after you die. By the way, Satan is not impressed, even if you worship him. He may shower you with riches or make your life a living Hell. Hell. Now there's a subject you may find yourself wondering about.

Furthermore, both the Old and the New testaments address loving the Lord God Almighty as the first commandment. And for those who still use the Lord's name in vain in their swearing vocabulary, and you know who you are, I would strongly recommend apologizing to God when you slip up and say it. And then make it a habit to just stop swearing altogether. Asking God for forgiveness for *any* slights and making this a part of your prayer life will increase the quantity of casual miracles you experience.

What if you don't repent of your sins asking Jesus to be your personal Lord and Savior? That depends on who you ask. If God is love, would He send you to Hell for all eternity? What of all those people who died in the Old Testament before Jesus ever died on the Cross and rose again? It's true that Jesus is the Way to eternal life. But if you never accept Him into your heart, what then? Do you just never wake up when Jesus comes back? These are questions you now don't have to worry about do you? For at this very moment, you can assure your future destiny with Him and everyone else who has given their lives to Him. Don't put it off any longer. Not even for a second. Ask Him into your heart right now by praying the sinner's prayer. It can be found at the end of this book on page 92.

Jesus was a real person and is real, as real as you and me. And when they rolled away the stone door at His tomb and looked inside, well, it was empty. So, ask yourself this, "where did He go?" That (along with everything else I've said), is reason enough for me to believe what the Bible teaches. No other so-called prophets have been able to escape death and disappear from their tombs, have they? So, on that point alone, I choose Christ. The Son of God. And everything the Bible teaches. And ONLY the Bible.

This is my testimony.

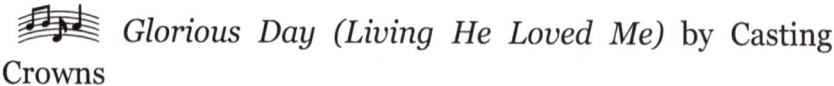 *Glorious Day (Living He Loved Me)* by Casting Crowns

A Little More Proof

On what basis should the Bible be considered trustworthy and authoritative? The reason to trust the Bible is because it is God's Word. *All scripture is given by inspiration of God* (2 Timothy 3:16). Also see: 2 Peter 1:20-21 for further study.

However, to further convince those skeptics, and you know who you are, more evidence is supplied below. I am providing the resources and leaving the digging up to you.

By proving the Bible real, this allows me to cite from it as from any historical document/history book; quoting from its many authors, (about 40 in all over 1,600 years), which I have done throughout this book - quoting chapter and verse. I have eased your burden of gathering the many resources and listed them here. Any one of the listed resources is sufficient and stands on its own to prove the Bible as a viable document. I encourage you to choose any that peak your interest and explore it to the depth necessary to both satisfy and convince you that the Bible is God's infallible Word and can be trusted and hence should be used as the sole source calling you to live an eternal life with Him.

Do not make the mistake of setting it aside out of spite and losing out on the promises it offers! You can also download the Bible Gateway App onto your cellphone or tablet and have up to 56 different versions, commentaries, devotionals, dictionaries, encyclopedias, and sermons at your disposal.

Once you are convinced of its reality, turn immediately to part VII of this book and pray the Sinner's Prayer and be welcomed to the family!

Pray. Get quiet and trust that "something" is out there. I guarantee you that a sense of peace will overcome you that you have never felt before. That, to me, is proof. What's more is, that whatever you prayed for may just happen. What are you going to say when/if that occurs? Coincidence? I think not. So, do it again tomorrow. See how many prayers it takes for you to start thinking… "hey, maybe there's something to this after all."

If, when you pray, you feel more at peace, then couldn't that mean God exists? And if God exists, then couldn't that mean that the Bible is real? Something to ponder. By the way, and as a side note, the word Bible, means "the books." I prefer the often-used acronym:

<u>B</u>asic <u>I</u>nstructions <u>B</u>efore <u>L</u>eaving <u>E</u>arth

Something else to ponder.

Now when you pray, be certain to pray using the language of God. You inherently know it. It's called *faith*. That's the language God speaks. If it weren't so, there wouldn't be so many verses regarding it in the Bible. *Therefore, I tell you, whatever you ask for in prayer, believe that you have received it, and it will be yours.* (NIV) Mark 11:24. Or, *for we live by faith, not by sight.* (NIV) 2 Corinthians 5:7.

God asks us to take the leap of faith and trust in Him to catch us; not the other way around. I know it's hard, but trust me, He will catch you. He always has and He always will.

🎵 *Faith* by Jordan Feliz

Oh, and hey. No one needs to know about your secret belief except you & God. So, don't worry what your friends will think. Besides, if your "friends" are really going to judge you for trying this God thing out, well, who needs judgmental friends anyway? The only person I want judging me is God. Pleasing Him has made my life incredible! All kinds of unexplainable things have come together in my life. It even says that in.... the Bible.

"For all good things come together for those who love Christ." – Romans 8:28

In order to get around the argument of proving the Bible is real and thus useful, as I have done, I point you to these resources. Invest the price of a large pizza or a portion of your tithe—if you have one—and acquire one or more of the following. I have underlined sources discussing archaeological digs where they find items that are discussed in the Bible. That alone, supplies evidence proving the Bible is a historical document and can be relied upon as such. So, the only question you really should be asking yourself is this: Which Bible version are you going to buy? (For a suggestion, see #10 below.) The blue underlines are links you can enter manually (or wait for the eBook version to click on).

1. Is Genesis History at https://isgenesishistory.com/ - fascinating new evidence for creation and a global flood.

2. Patterns of Evidence: The Exodus at https://patternsofevidence.com/ - as people are questioning the validity of the Bible, this film supports the truth of the Bible.
3. Christ Revealed at https://www.christrevealed.com/ - gives a solid body of evidence as to the authenticity of Christ's life, identity, and teachings.
4. Museum of the Bible - at https://museumofthebible.org/ - located just three blocks from the U.S. Capitol in Washington, D.C. Museum of the Bible aims to be among the most technologically advanced and engaging museums in the world. Showcasing rare and fascinating artifacts spanning 3,500 years of history, the museum offers visitors an immersive and personalized experience with the Bible. Highlighting the ancient texts of the Bible using some of the most engaging technology available; with many top-tier, award-winning exhibits, you are sure to engage with the Bible in a whole new way!
5. The Amazing Bible Timeline Chart at https://amazingbibletimeline.com/ - easily see over 6,000 years of Biblical and world history together!
6. Handbook's to the Bible – These *handbooks* are well thought out, deeply researched Bible commentaries including hundreds of full-color images, drawings, and maps; important discoveries in archaeology, related historical data, church history, historical geography, and more. Whether you've read the Bible many times or never before, you will find insights that give you a firm grasp of God's Word and an appreciation for the cultural, religious, and geographic settings in which the story of the Bible unfolds. Written for both mind and heart for all ages 5 and up, they feature:
    - Maps, photographs, and illustrations
    - Contemporary design
    - Practical Bible reading programs
    - Helpful tips for Bible study
    - Fascinating archaeological information

- Easy-to-understand sections on <u>how we got the Bible</u> and on church history
- <u>Archeological evidence</u> to support the events and places mentioned.

➤ Zondervan Handbook to the Bible, 5th Edition, by David and Pat Alexander (816 pages in softback) is an indispensable piece of biblical literature.

➤ Halley's Bible Handbook **Deluxe** Edition by Henry H. Halley, 25th edition (1,047 pages in hardback)

7. https://www.thegreatcourses.com/courses/dead-sea-scrolls.html#BVRRWidgetID – The Dead Sea Scrolls offered by The Great Courses and taught by Professor Gary A. Rendsburg, Ph.D. In this course, you'll discover:

➤ In 1947 a Bedouin shepherd tracks one of his stray goats into a cave mouth above the shore of the Dead Sea at a desolate place named Qumran. Inside, he discovers a pair of tall, thin clay pots. And what he finds when he opens those pots will be nothing less than the greatest <u>archaeological</u> discovery of the 20th century: The Dead Sea Scrolls.

➤ In the 60 years, (the original 7 scrolls this Bedouin shepherd uncovered grew to 930 scrolls) since their dramatic discovery, excavation, reassembly, and translation, the Dead Sea Scrolls have provided us with these and other fascinating insights:

1. Our oldest biblical manuscripts, including all of the book of Isaiah, portions of virtually every other book in the Hebrew Bible, and other texts esteemed by ancient Jews.
2. An unprecedented window into two great monotheistic traditions in the pivotal years before and after the time of Jesus, offering insights into Jewish history, culture, and religion, as well as the growth of early Christianity out of Judaism.

3. Enhanced knowledge of how the Bible was transmitted across the ages
   - Throughout the course, you spend a wealth of time reading parts of the actual scrolls in English translation.
   - By the conclusion of the final lecture, you'll have developed a newfound understanding and appreciation of an unprecedented historical find and its enduring influence on the way we think about—and talk about—ancient Judaism and Christianity.
8. Now, about all those angel sightings. I've read a couple of books where people wanted to give thanks to "who was that person that helped me…." and no one was around to thank!
   - Angels Among Us, Encounters with Heavenly Beings by Wanda Rosseland; Worthy Publishing Group "Helping people experience the heart of God"
   - Celebration of Angels, A compelling look at the heavenly beings who touch our lives, by Timothy Jones. Thomas Nelson Publishers
   - Chicken Soup for the Soul: Angels Among Us: 101 Inspirational Stories of Miracles, Faith, and Answered Prayers, by Jack Canfield, Mark Victor Hansen, and Amy Newmark. Chicken Soup for the Soul Publishing, LLC
   - To better understand the 3rd of the Angels/Demons who were kicked out of Heaven along with Satan/Lucifer, I invite you read Frank E. Peretti, an entertaining author who writes fiction and paints a realistic view of the dark side.
9. Take a tour of the Holy Land on foot. Walk where Jesus walked See: https://walkingthetext.com/ Shy of that, be sure to download the **most excellent resource,** a free 33 page eBook (and perhaps print it out) "The #1 Mistake Most Everyone Makes Reading the Bible."

- Over 300 <u>excavations</u> take place every year in Israel matching up to what the Bible says. "Jesus isn't a fable, and neither was what He did." Brad Gray
- See the evidence of where the revolution took place to walk in Jesus' actual footsteps. Visit Israel.

10. NIV Life Application Study Bible

Let There be Music... ♪

There is a plethora of songs which could in themselves be sufficient in moving you into a place of worship and willingness to accept the Bible as God's infallible written Word. "Christian music lifts you up and tells us a better day is coming and there's a God who loves us and there's a God who cares." – The Jesus Music, KLOVE Books.

KLOVE.com and other Christian radio stations play continuous music that, in itself, could move you to belief. In addition to all the songs displayed throughout this book, the following are added for your edification, enjoyment, playlist... and perhaps even chill-inducing!

- ✞ Hillsong Worship, "Who You Say I am"
- ✞ Newsboys, "God's Not Dead"
- ✞ Rich Mullens, "Creed" "Awesome God" "Step by Step"
- ✞ Twila Paris, "God Is in Control"
- ✞ Carman, "Awesome God" & *The Standard* LP
- ✞ Steven Curtis Chapman, "The Great Adventure" "Dive"
- ✞ Michael W. Smith, "Place in This World"
- ✞ Chris Tomlin, "How Great Is Our God" & "Our God"
- ✞ Mercy Me, "Word of God Speak"
- ✞ Casting Crowns, "Glorious Day (Living He Loved Me)"
- ✞ Chris Rice, "Cartoons"
- ✞ Amy Grant, "Sing Your Praise to the Lord" & the entire *The Collection* LP
- ✞ Mark Schultz, "I Am"
- ✞ Third Day, "God of Wonders"
- ✞ Lincoln Brewster, "Everlasting God"
- ✞ Wayne Watson, "Home Free, the Ultimate Healing"

- ☨ Jars of Clay, "I'll Fly Away"
- ☨ Avalon, "Testify To Love" & *the very best of* LP
- ☨ Petra, "Love" & the entire *Beyond Belief* LP
- ☨ Maranatha! Music, "Change My Heart Oh God"
- ☨ Darlene Zschech, "The Power of Your Love"
- ☨ Hillary Scott & The Scott Family, "Thy Will"
- ☨ Carrie Underwood w/Vince Gill, "How Great Thou Art"
- ☨ Jeremy Camp, "Here I Am To Worship" "I Still Believe"
- ☨ Matt Maher, "Lord, I Need You"
- ☨ We The Kingdom, "Holy Water"
- ☨ Jaci Velasquez, "God So Loved"
- ☨ David Crowder Band, "How He Loves"
- ☨ Lauren Daigle, "Still Rolling Stones"
- ☨ Carrollton, "Leaning In" on Everything or Nothing LP
- ☨ CeCe Winans, "Believe For It"
- ☨ Needtobreathe, "Who Am I"
- ☨ Dave Barnes, "God Gave Me You"

Why wait to hear these amazing, life-changing songs? Purchase or pull them up on your favorite streaming app such as Spotify, Pandora, iTunes, or even YouTube.com and prepare to be ***moved*** beyond Heaven & Earth. You will also find more songs and your familiarization with them being sung in your local Church. Feel free to lift your hands in worship. You won't be alone.

*There are so many great songs, I wish I could include them all! However, due to space considerations, selection was purely randomized, and the choices made consistent with this book's content. I encourage my readers to compile their playlist based on *their* personal tastes and preferences. My apologies to those amazing artists and their remarkable songs who could not be included on this list. For an A to Z listing of artists, please visit https://www.klove.com/music/artists

Part VI

The Power of the Holy Spirit

Once you have prayed the "Sinner's Prayer" and have accepted Jesus into your heart by making Him your personal Lord and Savior, you will receive eternal life. What that means is your body will age but your spirit will go to Heaven after you die living with Jesus and everyone else who has given their life to Him, too. You might even find that a better version of yourself is what your spirit lives in, in Heaven. After you have prayed the "Sinner's Prayer" you are born again. The first time you were born was from your mother's womb. Hence the term "born-again".

But that is not all that happens when you give your life to Jesus. You also receive the gift of the Holy Spirit. Your body literally becomes a "temple housing the Spirit of God (1 Corinthians 6:19). So, take good care of it. Of course, you still have free-will. You can go on living just like you were right up until you gave your life to Jesus. But why would you want to? You now have a new best friend who will never leave you nor forsake you. As you are about to discover, you have powers you probably never knew existed. So, let's get to it.

By way of the Holy Spirit indwelling or living within you, you have two new attributes: they are the Fruits and the Gifts. Let us touch first on the *Fruits*, which are given to us to improve our character, and can be found in Galatians 5:22:

Spiritual Fruits

1. Love
2. Joy
3. Peace
4. Patience
5. Kindness
6. Goodness
7. Faithfulness
8. Gentleness
9. Self-control

You might just want to memorize these because they are yours. And it will help you to live them. See why, now, you may just want to change? The Bible goes on to say, *against such things, there is no law. Those who belong to Christ Jesus have crucified the sinful nature with its passions and desires. Since we live by the Spirit, let us keep in step with the Spirit. Let us not become conceited, provoking and envying each other.*

Read the rest of Galatians. It is not long and will answer many of your questions.

The Strong's Lexicon defines each this way:

Love (*Agape*) - an undefeatable benevolence and unconquerable goodwill that always seeks the highest good for others, no matter their behavior. It is a love that gives freely without asking anything in return.

Joy - deeper than mere happiness; it is rooted in God and comes from Him. Since it comes from God, it is more serene and stable than worldly happiness, which is merely emotional and lasts only for a time.

Peace - expresses the idea of wholeness, completeness, or tranquility in the soul that is unaffected by outward circumstances or pressures.

Patience - the power to exercise revenge but instead exercises restraint.

Kindness - acting for the good of people regardless of what they do.

Goodness - is an example of moral excellence and virtue.

Faithfulness - being trustworthy <u>and</u> trustful, being sure, being true.

Gentleness - even-tempered, tranquil, balanced in spirit, unpretentious, with passions under control.

Self-control - having mastery over one's thoughts and actions.

Having discussed the Fruits, let us now touch on the Gifts...

Spiritual Gifts

1 Corinthians 12:4-6 tells us *There are different kinds of gifts, but the same Spirit distributes them. There are different kinds of service, but the same Lord. There are different kinds of working, but in all of them and in everyone it is the same God at work.*

Unlike the *fruits* mentioned above, which are given to us to improve our own individual character, the gifts are given to us for the purpose of service to others. Not every Christian has every gift, but they are sorted out as the Christian body needs them, as determined by the Holy Spirit. The purpose of the gifts is to build up, encourage, and comfort the church (body of Christ).

The gifts are broken down into three categories:

1. Manifestation
2. Ministry
3. Motivation

The Manifestation gifts (1 Corinthians 12:7-11) are:

1. Wisdom - the gift of wise words
2. Knowledge - insight into a given situation without having been told
3. Faith - trusting God
4. Healing - physical, spiritual, and psychological
5. Powers - literally 'acts of power'

6. Prophecy - speaking directly from God to uplift other people
7. Distinguishing between spirits - capacity to "discern" a spirit, good or evil
8. Speaking in tongues - praising God with an unknown tongue
9. Interpretation of tongues - interpreting the unknown tongue

The Ministry Gifts (Ephesians 4:11-13) are:

1. Apostles
2. Prophets
3. Evangelists
4. Pastors
5. Teachers
6. Helpers (see 1 Corinthians 12:28)

The Motivation Gifts (Romans 12:6-8) are:

1. Prophesying
2. Serving
3. Teaching
4. Encouraging
5. Giving
6. Leading
7. Showing mercy

Thus, ends our discussion on the Gifts.

What to Wear to the War?

What to wear to the war. War? What war? You know all those innocent cartoons, how there are always good guys and bad guys? Well, that's because, unfortunately, that is the way the real-world works. Evil lurks around every corner. And it has been that way since the beginning. It was Satan who lured Eve into biting the forbidden fruit from the tree of knowledge of good and evil. And you need to know about this: So, don't worry, we are going to borrow from the above illustration and use them to equip ourselves to win the war against Satan. We know how the final battle turns out. We win! See Revelation, the 66th chapter in the Bible. That is why it is imperative that you and everyone you know turns to Christ! Because it's

Satan's intention to keep everyone from knowing the truth and especially from becoming a Christian. Why do you think it can be so hard! We are in nothing less than a war. Otherwise, it would be easy. But now you know (so you have no excuse). Don't fret, God has already equipped you with the armor you need.

What I am going to share with you can be found in Ephesians 6:10-20 *The Armor of God*. Which, like a lot of the Bible is a simile. It is *not* an actual suit of armor like most of us have been led to picture.

My understanding is that Satan, that is, the Devil cannot read your mind. He is only an angel, albeit a powerful one. He is also called Lucifer, the angel of light. He was kicked out of Heaven and took a third of the angels with him. These are called demons and they are the ones who wreak havoc with us down here on Earth. All the bad stuff that goes on is most likely a result of them. Satan's weapons are to divide, denounce, destroy, doubt, defeat, discourage, and deny. However, we as Christians, are more than equipped since we have the whole armor of God.

We also have the remaining angels to help keep us safe. You have read about angelic encounters, or you should. There are plenty of books on the subject you can acquire to read. They are very uplifting and referenced in Part V of this book as additional proof of the Bible's truthfulness. God and his angels can be counted on to protect His flock. As a born-again Christian, you have an arsenal from which to use to protect both yourself and those whom you love.

The Whole Armor of God

The whole armor of God is a simile used in the Bible to illustrate our defenses and each are mentioned throughout the Old and New Testament yet summarized by Paul here as follows in verses contained in Ephesians 6:10-20.

> *11: Put on the full armor of God...to stand firm against the schemes of the devil.*
>
> *12: For our struggle is not against flesh and blood...but against spiritual forces in the heavenly places.*
>
> *14: Stand firm...having girded your loins with **truth** and having put on the breastplate of **righteousness**.*
>
> *15: having shod your feet with the preparation of the **gospel of peace**.*
>
> *16: ...taking up the shield of **faith**...to extinguish the flaming arrows of the evil one.*
>
> *17: and take the helmet of **salvation** and the sword of the Spirit, which is the **word of God**.*

I've found an explanation of each "tool" is helpful...

> The girdle, or belt of **truth,** keeps us from being double-minded and from serving two masters.
> See: James 1:8, John 17:17, John 8:32, and John 14:6.

The breastplate of **righteousness** reminds us we have been justified and made righteous in Christ.
See: Isaiah 59:16-17, 1 Corinthians 1:30

Wearing the shoes of the **gospel of peace** combats evil by doing good and is the antidote for war.
See: Isaiah 52:7, Romans 10:15

We need to use the shield of **faith** (the Word of God) to quench the fiery darts of doubt.
See: Genesis 15:1, Psalms 3:3, Hebrews 11 (The Faith Chapter)

We need to take the helmet of **salvation** to know of the blessed hope of Jesus Christ's return.
See: Isaiah 59:17,

The sword of the spirit is the **Word of God** which is sharper than any two-edged sword.
See: Heb 4:12

Prayer. This is another instrument (tool) in your arsenal. Pray. And pray often. Especially for strength and for your loved ones. Furthermore, keep a prayer journal handy and use it. That is also a powerful tool. One other tool which I've yet to mention is to stay strong by joining a church body.

 Church (Take Me Back) by Cochren & Co.

Find one which you feel comfortable going to regularly. They come in all sizes. Just be sure they put Jesus, the Son of God, first and recognize the Cross as the only way to salvation. I covered this in an earlier chapter. Satan would like to toss Jesus and the Cross He died on for you, out of the picture.

That is Satan's main thing because he knows Jesus defeated him on the Cross.

"I am the way, the truth and the life. No one comes to the Father except through me" – Jesus

Most importantly, know that you have the power to rebuke Satan by praying these words:

"I rebuke thee Satan, in the name of Jesus Christ!"

For greater is He that is in me than he that is in the world.
1 John 4:4

Part VII

The Ending

In order to be sure you start or continue to receive God's blessings, pray the Sinner's Prayer. The Bible says that if you confess with your mouth that Jesus is Lord and believe in your heart that God raised Him from the dead, *you will be saved.* For it is with your heart that you believe and are justified, and it is with your mouth that you confess and are saved. Everyone who calls on the name of the Lord will be saved. Pray this prayer out loud:

The Sinner's Prayer

Dear God, I am a sinner. I repent of my sins. I believe that Jesus died on the Cross and rose again in place of me for my sins and that God raised Him up from the dead. I ask Jesus to come into my life to be my personal Lord and Savior. Thank you, God. In Jesus precious name I pray. Amen.

Welcome to the family! A multitude of Angels are now singing in celebration. Jesus said, *In the same way, I tell you, there is rejoicing in the presence of the angels of God over one sinner who repents.* (Luke 15:10) You'll find the Biblical reference for the above prayer in Chapter 10 verses 9 & 10, of Romans, the sixth chapter of the New Testament.

🎵 *Creed* by Petra on Beyond Belief Album

Now that you have repented of your sins, it is important to continue confessing your sins often: for the Apostle Paul says in 1 Thessalonians to pray continually. Whenever I have a thought or action that I know is not right, I just say quickly to God, "Please forgive me". <u>This wipes the slate clean every time.</u> And you will get an immediate thought that sounds something like this *"I forgive you"*. or *"You are forgiven"*. You won't be able to deny it. It is between you and God. You will feel such a relief come over you that you will know it is undeniably from God. And you'll have a fresh start every time you do this for that which you asked. I think you need to do this for every wrongful act or thought in your life. Sure, you may feel like you'll never "catch up," but that is OK. You are human. And humans are always messing up. It is the confession that sets you free.

Try to be as specific as possible with sins. Know that God absolutely will forgive you. So, don't think that you are so far gone God won't forgive you. He will.

🎵 *The God Who Stays* by Matthew West

You will also receive the Fruit (Gal 5:22) and the Gifts (1 Corinthians 12-14) of the Holy Spirit. That is why I included a chapter in this book on what that means. Not only do you now have eternal life, but you are also blessed beyond measure while here on Earth. Tell your friends and especially your family so that they too can receive the Fruits and the Gifts and be part of your Heavenly family.

The, "I know there is something greater than myself," humbling yourself, is all God expects of you. Now you have availed yourself to receive His blessings. It really is that simple. And no one needs to know every sin you confess. So, go ahead. What have you to lose? Nothing. And everything to gain.

Now, tune into positive, encouraging KLOVE on your radio to continually cleanse your mind and edify your soul. You can find them on your radio dial, via the Klove app, Klove.com, or say "Alexa, play KLOVE." Or "Hey Google, play [the specific song title and artist]" For instance, "Hey Google, play *Angels* by Amy Grant."

One more thing is an assignment I strongly encourage you to do. Download the "Bible Gateway" App so that you can do what I do often. Listen first to the Gospel of John, the 4th book of the New Testament. You will learn why you must give your life to Jesus so you acquire the Holy Spirit. One, is that you cannot enter the Kingdom of God without it and two, so that you do not incur the wrath of God (Romans 5:9). Then, go on to listen to the entire Bible at your leisure. This is one uncomplicated way to get through the entire Bible in the shortest time frame.

🎵 I leave you with this song: *Well Done* by The Afters

The Priestly Blessing

The Lord bless you and keep you;
The Lord make His face shine upon you
and be gracious to you;
The Lord turn his face toward you
and give you peace.

 The Blessing, Kari Jobe, Cody Carnes

Numbers 6:24-26

References & Resources

Scriptures are taken from various Bibles – Public Domain

Walter Martin, *The Kingdom of the Cults*

Josh McDowell, *Evidence That Demands A Verdict* and *More Than A Carpenter*

Warren W. Wiersbe, *What To Wear To The War, Studies from Ephesians 6*

https://www.biblica.com/

https://www.bitesizedtruth.com/thomas-paine-God-science/

https://www.klove.com/

App: Bible Gateway Plus, Harper Collins Christian Publishing LLC

http://www.Godsaidmansaid.com/

Is Genesis History at https://isgenesishistory.com/

Patterns of Evidence: The Exodus at https://patternsofevidence.com/

Christ Revealed at https://www.christrevealed.com/

https://walkingthetext.com/

Zondervan Handbook to the Bible, 5th Edition, by David and Pat Alexander

Halley's Bible Handbook **Deluxe** Edition by Henry H. Halley, 25th edition

The Jesus Music, Marshall Terrill, KLOVE BOOKS, 2021

Suicide Prevention: 1-800-282-8255 (talk)

www.ingramcontent.com/pod-product-compliance
Lightning Source LLC
Chambersburg PA
CBHW071306040426
42444CB00009B/1893